Is the War Over?

Also by R. Gabriele S. Silten

Dark Shadows, Bright Life
Between Two Worlds
High Tower Crumbling

Is the War Over?

R. Gabriele S. Silten

2004 · FITHIAN PRESS
MCKINLEYVILLE, CALIFORNIA

Published by Fithian Press
A division of Daniel and Daniel, Publishers, Inc.
Post Office Box 2790
McKinleyville, CA 95519
www.danielpublishing.com

LIBRARY OF CONGRESS CATALOGING-IN-PUBLICATION DATA
Silten, R. Gabriele S., (date)
  Is the war over : memoir of a child survivor of the Holocaust / Silten R. Gab-
rielle S.
    p. cm.
  ISBN 1-56474-429-9 (pbk. : alk. paper)
  1. Silten, R. Gabriele S., (date) 2. Silten, R. Gabriele S., 1933—Childhood
and youth. 3. Jews, German—Netherlands—Amsterdam—Biography.
4. Holocaust survivors—Netherlands—Amsterdam—Biography.
5. Jews, German United States—Biography. 6. Holocaust survivors—
United States—Biography. 7. Amsterdam (Netherlands)—Biography.
8. United States—Biography. I. Title.
  DS135.N6S562 2003
  940.53'18'092—dc21
          2003003987

IN MEMORIAM

this is for my beloved Mami, Papi,
and Tante Ulle.

You loved me with unconditional love,
as I loved you. I will always love you.
You are always with me.
The memory of you
is a blessing.

Acknowledgements

Many warm thanks go to those who, in one way or another, have helped and encouraged me in this work. Many thanks and hugs to my dear friend Maryon Leonard, who encouraged me at every step, then proofread the manuscript and gave me helpful comments. Thanks and a hug also go to my friend Lainie Lapis, who read the manuscript and had very helpful questions and suggestions. And to the one who pushed me to begin this book, my friend Ursula Duba, I owe more thanks than I know how to express. Without her determined pushing, I probably would not have written this work. So, my warmest thanks to all of you and hugs all around. I am happy and grateful that you are my friends.

Contents

Some Pre-Prologue Words 11

Prologue 19

Homecoming 25

In Carla's Apartment 29

Language Changes and Silence 35

Elementary School 43

Manners 51

Denmark 57

Het Amsterdams Lyceum 71

Ends of a Childhood 77

Emotions 85

CARE Packages and Other Things 91

Trip to Lugano 95

Edith 103

Teenage Years 111

Dancing Lessons and Other Problems 121

Bad Gastein 125

England 129

Geneva 133

Return to Amsterdam 141

To the United States of America 145

My First Job 149

The In Between Years 153

Trouble 157

The Later Years 163

Residuals—The Present 167

Important Things Today 177

Is the War Over? 185

Epilogue 195

What Happened to Whom? 197

Glossary 201

Some Pre-Prologue Words

This will be just a shortish introduction to explain where I come from and what my upbringing was like. It explains many things in this book.

I was born in Berlin, Germany, as were my parents and grandparents and many generations before them. That means that my ancestors had been living in what is now called Germany for centuries before the Enlightenment which started in the late 18th century. The Enlightenment, also known in Hebrew as *Haskalah*, is described in *The Jewish Information Source Book* (Ronald H. Isaacs; Jason Aronson Inc. Publishing, 1993) as follows: "It refers to the 18th-century movement for spreading modern European culture among Jews." The founder of this movement was Moses Mendelsohn (1729-1786). The *Book of Jewish Knowledge* (Nathan Ausubel; Crown Publishers, Inc., 1964) says the following: "He (Moses Mendelsohn) realized that in the general spread of free ideas, laws and institutions—which would involve the exercise of freedom of conscience and a separation of Church and State—Jews, for the first time, would be able to come into their own and stand on an equal footing with Christians. Almost a century later, in observing the rosy social and cultural landscape of Jewish life in Germany, the historian of German literature, Ludwig W. Geiger, saluted Mendelsohn as the Father of the Berlin Haskalah."

Because of this Enlightenment and the equality of Christians and Jews, both my paternal and maternal grandparents, like so many other German Jews, considered themselves Germans, first and foremost. They were totally assimilated. Though they knew that they were Jewish, they did not practice Judaism, i.e., they did not keep the dietary laws, did not go to synagogue, did not observe any of the Holy Days and holidays. My parents, then, were brought up as Germans and not as Jews. When, from the early 1920's, discrimination began anew against Jews, my grandparents and parents did not think of themselves as Jews, but as Germans. Therefore nothing could or would happen to them. My parents had a German upbringing which they, naturally, passed on to me. It is a manner of child rearing which is rather out of fashion today, at least here in the USA and in many other countries as well. It was the time of children being seen but not heard, of doing what any adult told the child to do, of obeying the parents. It was *not* a time of discussions, talking back, protest by children; it was also *not* a time in which children asked many questions or parents provided many explanations. What the adults said, went; there was no question about that. Parents did not express *their* feelings to their children and therefore children did not express *their* feelings towards their parents. Children, and thus also I, were taught to have self-discipline and self-control; we were taught not to complain, especially about small matters. In later years, when I had pain somewhere, one of my parents would say: "Millions of people have the same pain. Don't think about it. Don't talk about it."

When Hitler came to power in 1933 and continued the discrimination against Jews, the German Jews began to find out that the equality they had so treasured no longer existed. It no longer mattered that people considered themselves German and not Jewish, or that they were assimilated; the Nuremberg laws made this impossible. Effective September 15, 1935, these laws stated that even a person with one-quarter "Jewish blood" was a Jew and was not to be considered German, no matter how the person thought of himself. This then meant that Jews felt that the discrimination against them was, in fact, a discrimination of Germans against Germans. Many Jews left Germany, many members of my family went to then Palestine (now Israel), to England, to Denmark and to Latin America. My parents and I also left. We left behind my maternal grandmother (my maternal grandfather had died before my parents were married) and both my paternal grandparents. We left behind also practically all we possessed, such as furniture, clothing, toys for me (I was five years old when we left) and so on. We emigrated to flee Nazism, in 1938, and went to Amsterdam, Holland. My paternal grandmother joined us in 1939. In May of 1940 the Germans invaded Holland, as they did many other countries, and from then on Holland was an occupied territory. As such it was subject to all the same laws and regulations which were in effect in Germany. In June of 1943, the four of us were deported to Westerbork, a concentration camp in Holland and from there, in January 1944, to Theresienstadt, a concentration camp in Czechoslovakia. We were liberated by the Russian army on May 8, 1945 and eventually returned to Amsterdam.

Ernst Silten
B. Apr 22, 1866
D. Mar 5, 1943

Marta Silten
(*née* Friedberg)
B. Oct. 12, 1877
D. July 7, 1943

Richard Teppich
B. Jun 27, 1869
D. Jul 18, 1931

Gertrud Teppich
(*née* Herz)
B. Feb 12, 1880
D. Nov 8, 1942

M. March 15, 1900

M. October 14, 1903

Heinz (Henry) Silten
B. Jun 11, 1901
D. Mar 13, 1953

Fritz Silten
B. Feb 16, 1904
D. Nov 15, 1980

Ilse Silten
(*née* Teppich)
B. Feb 23, 1909
D. Feb 23, 1977

**Ursula (Ulle)
Teppich**
B. Dec 6, 1914
D. May 5, 1990

M. August 6, 1931

**Ruth Gabriele
Sarah Silten**
B. May 30, 1933

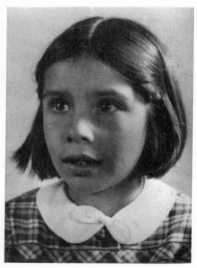

Top: Gabriele, 1938, age five.

Center: Gabriele, 1941, age eight.

Bottom: Gabriele, 1945, age twelve, directly after the concentration camps.

⌒ *Prologue*

In 1995, my first autobiography, *Between Two Worlds*, dealing with my childhood, was published. As I said in the foreword to that book, "my childhood and early teen years were spent in a sort of twilight zone. This book is going back in time and space to recapture what happened to me and thereby make my story public in an effort to do my small part to try and ensure that this type of genocide will never happen again."

Many people, over the years, have asked and are still asking: "How have your experiences affected your life today?" or "What was life like after the war was over?"

In this second book, I will try and answer these and other questions, mostly the one about what was life like in the years after "the war was over." How did we cope? How did we feel? What did we do? What did we think of? I can only speak for myself, of course, not for anyone else, not even for my parents who were adults where I was a child. In order to have some continuity from the earlier book to this one, I repeat here the last chapter of *Between Two Worlds*. I will then try and expand on this since that last chapter gives no details.

AFTER THE WAR

We stayed with our neighbors for a long time, probably at least a year. The winter of 1944–1945 was terrible in Holland. It was one of the coldest and cruelest winters on record, and there was no food to eat and no fuel for heating. The streets were denuded of trees, the parks had lost their trees and bushes. People used broken-up furniture and anything else that would burn in their stoves to have at least a little heat. During this last war winter, the Germans sent as much food as possible to Germany, with the result that practically nothing was left for the Dutch. That winter has gone down in history as the *Hongerwinter*, the Hungerwinter, when people died in the streets of starvation, when they ate not only their cats and dogs, but also whatever rats and mice they could catch. They ate tulip bulbs cooked in various ways: tulip bulb meatloaf, tulip bulb stew, tulip bulb cakes. If they were really lucky, there was some grass to go with it all. When at last the liberators came and brought with them powdered eggs, powdered milk, chocolate and all sorts of food, the Dutch were finally saved from total starvation. We did have rationing after the war, in fact for many years after the war, but nothing much was available. Sure, we had coupons for meat and eggs, but we couldn't buy any, for there weren't any to buy. Under those circumstances, when a family already has two children; then to take in another starving family of three, one of whom is a child, is nothing less than heroic. Yet that is what Carla's family did. Somehow they stretched what food there was; somehow they made it serve seven instead of four. Somehow they fed all of us.

Carla's family also reported to the police the woman who was in our former apartment and who was a member of the Nationaal Socialistische Bond, the Dutch Nazi party, and a collaborator. She was taken to prison, and we were able to rent the same apartment we had before the war.

Eventually, in August 1945, Elementary School started again, and I had to go back to school. At first I was afraid; I had missed two years, after all. I soon found out, however, that everyone was in the same boat. The children in my fifth grade class ranged in age from about eleven to about sixteen years, having also missed school because of being in hiding or in concentration camps or for various other reasons. Over the next few years I tried hard to catch up; I was able to pass from one grade to the next without having to repeat any.

Slowly but surely life returned to normal, especially after all three of us were once again in our own apartment. Normal? No, not really normal. Too many people had "not come back"—i.e. had not survived; too many scars, both physical and psychic, remained—and remain even today. Too many ghosts surround us. But as my friend Carla said in one of her recent letters, *You came back. True, you came back without Omi, but you came back. How on earth was all this possible?*

About a year ago, as of this writing, in March of 2001, the following online "conversation" took place between my friend Charlotte and me. She was in the same concentration camp as I (Theresienstadt as we know it or Terezín, the Czech name), but because of the difference in our ages, we did not know each other there. This conversation gives a small insight into what we feel and how we live today. Charlotte wrote the following:

Almost sixty years ago, I was informed that I would have to leave my world and join millions of other Jews in a place that, first off, required my falling down a certain rabbit hole called concentration camp. No matter how hard I try, I have never been able to see daylight again.

After several years in this venue, I was told that I could climb out, rejoin the human race and would be a free and normal human being again from that moment on.

I was informed that the brave Soviet Army and certain other soldiers had defeated all the German soldiers nearby, and life would be normal and sane once again.

I found that to be totally untrue.

At various and different times, I have tried to peek at this world and re-join the so-called normal people, but it is an insurmountable task. Lately I have observed that this so-called normal world is much strange and even more absurd and bizarre than the life with my friends in the rabbit hole.

There are perfectly normal people who CLAIM to have been with me and my friends—but they are only pretending. One of these people wrote a book about his experiences, but he was only telling stories.

Another man, a historian, claims that there were no rabbit holes and no concentration camps. He writes learned books, has many friends and gives lectures stating that all the things I have seen and heard with my eyes and ears did not happen.

I find all this very confusing. Will someone please show me the way out of this "normal" world and back to my rabbit hole?

I answered Charlotte's post and wrote in my turn:

I am very much afraid, Charlotte, that we, who were in the rabbit hole, will never be able to leave it. Like you, I find the "normal" world rather strange (and that is an understatement) and find people who can pretend—and seriously, mind you—that rabbit holes didn't exist, even stranger. I think that it is an insurmountable task to live, as we "rabbit-holers" do, in two worlds, neither of which is normal— whatever "normal" is. Whether we can ever succeed in such living, remains to be seen.

In this new book, I would like to describe, as best I can, what I felt during those post-war years and why I say that too many scars remain even today. I have relied on my memory, and have reconstructed conversations between my parents and me and between friends and me. This, then, is not a book of "verifiable facts"; it is strictly a book of memories, feelings, and what I today call "idiosyncrasies," i.e., reactions to things seen, heard, smelled even today.

Is the War Over?

⌒ *Homecoming*

June 1945. I am twelve years old. That is: I am twelve going on eight and I am also twelve going on a hundred and fifty. Both of those persons reside in me and come out at different times. Am I a child? Of course—at twelve years old, especially at that time in Europe, I was definitely a child. But I was also, at the very same time, a very old woman, far older than I will ever become in reality. Reality? What's that? Reality is that I am twelve; reality is also that I am eight and that I am a hundred and fifty. My parents and I have just spent three years in war conditions and two years in Nazi concentration camps, from June 1943 until liberation in May 1945. Then we had to stay until the typhus epidemic was over and transportation home could be found. We were taken to Eindhoven (in Holland) where we stayed for a week, until people found out where we could go. Now, finally we have come home. The camps were reality. The homecoming is reality. Reality is, probably, what I feel at any given moment.

Home? What is home? What does that mean? Is Holland home? We are back in Holland now and, oh joy, everyone speaks Dutch, not the hated German. Dutch is so much softer in my ears, it has all the familiar sounds which I love. There is no more "barking," no more:

"schnell, schnell," hurry, hurry. Even the sky is glad that we are back; it is as blue as blue can be with just a few small white clouds. It smiles at our homecoming. I wish I could smile. But I don't know how, I can't remember. The war years have been too long and in the camps there was nothing to smile about. How does one smile? Why does one smile?

They drove us home to Amsterdam in a truck. That was scary; when they deported us, it was in a truck also. But it turned out all right, this time. Is Amsterdam home? We go to Carla's family, in the apartment above ours from before the war. They greet us with lots of hugs. Does that mean home?

"They" were a group of people who had received us in Eindhoven. Were they volunteers? Were they a committee? Had they come of their own accord? I did not know then; I do not know now. To me they were just people I didn't know, adults who had the power of all adults to tell me what to do and where to go.

Everyone says "Welcome home," but that doesn't explain anything to me. Nobody explains "home" to me; I am left on my own to reason it out, if I can. First we see Carla's family, then the neighbors come to greet us, and even the lady from the corner grocery, Mevrouw Gijtenbeek, Mrs. Gijtenbeek, comes over to hug me and shake my parents' hands.

Now what do I do? I don't know whether I should say anything or not. Maybe it's better to just stay silent? They don't, at least, ask me any questions, so I don't have to answer. I don't know what to say, anyway. Should I stay in the room? If not, where should I go? We don't know yet how and where we sleep. Maybe, if I stay in the room but don't move, they won't see me. I'll be invisible. That would be good.

In the end I stay with the grown-ups but say nothing. Nobody notices me anyway and as long as I don't say anything, they won't either. That is the safest way. It's always safer if I am not noticed. Eventually they show us where we can sleep. And so life in freedom begins—but with a lot of questions and unknowns remaining, the first of which was: *What is freedom?* People tell us, my parents and me, that we are "free" now. But I don't know what that means. I am not really free. No child of twelve is really free. I have to stay with my parents and we all have to stay with Carla's family because we have no other place to go. I have to do what my parents say. I have to listen when they speak to me. I have to eat when they tell me to and what they tell me to. The things I used to do are now forbidden. So I don't really know what "freedom" means.

I was, as were we all, underweight and also small for my age; I didn't look more than about eight years old. I thought that that was a big flaw in me, probably because I was a Jew. There had been so many laws made against the Jews, we were allowed to do very few things and we were not allowed to do so many things. We couldn't go where we wanted to. Then we were deported to concentration camps. Being a Jew was obviously bad or else why would the Nazis have put us in concentration camps? In my view, I had a lot of flaws, although some of them would not show up till later. My main flaw, besides being Jewish, was that I was ugly—at least in my own eyes.

⌒ *In Carla's Apartment*

When we arrived in Amsterdam, after the week in Eindhoven, the whole city was decorated and there was a big celebration. The Dutch, the immigrants, everyone was happy to have the war over and the Germans gone. Oom Wim, Uncle Wim, took me down to the street to see whether we could find his daughter Carla who was out there somewhere. Indeed we did find her; Carla and a friend we had in common, another neighbor, named Anneke. They both received me with warm hugs. Then Carla asked:

How was it in the camp?

But I cannot answer; I can only shrug my shoulders.

I can't tell them about hunger; they were just as hungry. I can't explain what it's like to be always on your guard because you're afraid to get punished. How can I talk about waking up next to a dead person? How can I tell about the dead being everywhere around me? How can I talk about fleas and lice and bedbugs when they didn't have any and maybe don't even know what they look like?

So I just keep quiet and shrug my shoulders as an answer to that question. I have forgotten what life outside the camps was like and, in any event, could not yet—and not for many years to come—talk about the camps and what existence was like there.

Carla's apartment was identical to the one we had before

the war: it had a big living room, an equally big dining room, two bedrooms, also big, a kitchen and a bathroom. The living room and the dining room were connected and could be separated by closing a sliding glass door. There was an attic with several rooms. It was a little different from the attic of our apartment in that it had a big room (as did ours) and a small one which was furnished as a bedroom, as ours did not. In that small room we were to sleep. It was about as small as our last room in Theresienstadt had been and we—my parents and I—were a little crowded in it. But we were used to it; in Theresienstadt we had slept either in a biggish room with fifty others or in a smaller one which we had not quite to ourselves since a mother with her young son slept there as well. That first night when I went up to sleep, I marvelled:

Oooooh, look, the bed has sheets and they are soft and clean and white. And the mattress is not filled with straw! There is a pillow, too. What luxury—I can hardly believe it. And TWO blankets, nice, heavy ones. Are they wool? The one we had in Theresienstadt was very thin. And, wonder above wonder, there are no fleas and no bed-bugs. It's unbelievable! This must be Heaven! It can't be real, can it?

It was very difficult to believe that such luxuries really, truly existed and that we, concentration camp inmates, actually were allowed to sleep like that. And so we slept in that bedroom for as long as we were with Carla's family. We were supposed now to "go back to normal." That was difficult, because what is "normal"? For me, as a then twelve/eight/one-hundred-and-fifty-year-old, "normal" was what I had lived through in the last two years in the camps and the previous three war years. And so, various things happened which, in later years, could be, and often were, considered funny. One day I came to my mother:

Mami, I have no more toilet paper. Do you have any? May I have some?

My mother looked at me with big, amazed eyes:

Did you not see it hanging in the toilet room? It's next to the toilet.

It was my turn to be amazed:

You mean that's for us to use? How much can I use? What if it runs out?

My mother answered:

Of course, it's for you to use; it's for all of us to use. You can use as much as you like. If the roll is finished, we will put another one up. How is it that you don't know that? Don't you remember how it was?

No, Mami, I don't remember at all; all I remember is that we could just use a very little bit in Westerbork and Theresienstadt and I remember that often we didn't have any at all.

To me, this was one of the first miracles of the homecoming: just imagine, as much toilet paper as you want: incredible!

One night, after I had gone to bed, I decided to play a game. The bed I slept in was a Murphy bed; it came out of the wall and, during the day, the blankets and other bed linens were held in place with straps. I decided to find out what it would be like to sleep under one of the straps; I thought it might be fun. So I fastened the strap over my chest and went to sleep. My parents, when they came up, were aghast: they thought I had tried to commit suicide by strangling myself with the strap. That was farthest from my mind—all it was to me was a game. The next day they talked to me about it: why had I wanted to strangle myself?

Strangle myself??????? What on earth makes you think that? The strap went over my chest, not over my throat! I have no intention of strangling myself!

I was really quite indignant about the whole thing because, to my mind, they had totally misunderstood me. Today, I can see not only what my parents thought but also why. A lot of people committed suicide after the war: they had lost their families, their friends had not come back and they were alone in the world, a world that, not too long ago, had not wanted them. It had not wanted me or my family either—but suicide had truly not occurred to me.

So short a time after the war, there were many things which were not yet available or possible. The apartment was in a block of apartment buildings. It was heated from the building in which the landlord lived and the hot water came from there also. For several years after the war, we had no hot water at all because there was no coal, therefore no water could be heated. So we could not take a bath or a shower; we could only wash at the sink. I didn't know the difference, in Westerbork and Theresienstadt we had had no hot or even warm water; there were no baths or showers for the inmates. So, for me, it wasn't any different. I had no memory of baths or showers or even warm water to wash with. When winter came, there was no heat; again, there was no coal, hence no heat. We simply wore extra clothes if we had them. Again, I had no memory of a warm place to live, of warm rooms or a warm apartment. I don't remember when coal became available again; I do remember that when we first had hot water again, we were already back in our own apartment, so it must have been about a year after war's end. We had it just once a week, on Saturday. If you wanted, then, to bathe, you had to take your bath early in the day, otherwise the hot water would all be gone, since everyone, in every apartment, in the whole block, wanted a bath. Generally we just washed at the sink; if I was lucky, my mother would heat a kettle of water on the stove and I could parcel it out bit by bit, pour it into the sink, add cold water and so have lukewarm water to wash with, instead of ice cold. My mother, being who she was, checked me after I had washed, to see whether I felt cool all over, a sign that cold water had touched me. If my skin felt warm, she would make me wash while she supervised!

Those were things which, to me, were not disturbing—I knew no better and took everything in stride. There were other things, however, which were disturbing. For one, the apartment below us, that is, the apartment where we had lived before the war, was now occupied by a woman who had belonged to the N.S.B., the Dutch Nazi Party. She had "received" the apartment after our deportation, or maybe she had just moved in. Since the apartments had fairly thin walls, one could easily hear what was going on in other apartments. I could hear the Nazi woman walk around, go from one room into another, use the bathroom and so on. Her presence was always there. Even though I did not know her or even met or saw her ever, I knew she was there and I knew what she was: one of the people who had wanted us Jews dead. Since no one told me any different, I was convinced that she still wanted us dead. I just didn't know how she would go about it. It really wasn't a question of "if" but of "when" for me. I expected her every day, any day, to come and take me away, or take my parents and me away, to an unknown fate, just as had happened two years earlier when we had been deported. Her presence made life very difficult. Carla's family had reported her to the police and eventually they did come, they did arrest her and took her to prison. Still, her presence remained firmly there because although the landlord let us rent the apartment again, we had no furniture and had to make do with what the Nazi woman had left behind when she went to prison. I had her bed in my room and slept in it every night. I had her table and her four chairs and everything else that she had left behind in the room which became once again mine after we moved back in. I did not get new furniture, furniture which was specifically for me, until my twenty-first birthday, almost ten years later. In the beginning, furniture was not available, there was simply none to buy. Later, when furniture became available, we couldn't afford it; my father had his job, true, but nobody, including us, had any money to spare. Money was needed for food, clothing and rent. Anything else was a luxury.

⌒ Language Changes and Silence

From right away after the war, the language changed. To talk about what had happened to us was taboo, at least in my house. I could not ask questions, could not ask for information.

Mami, have you heard if Hans has come back? Where is he? Do you know anything?

No, I don't know anything.

That was the standard answer: "*I don't know*" or, instead of an answer, there might be only silence and a sort of look that meant: "*Don't ask such questions.*" Even if my parents had heard or had found out what had happened, they did not tell me. So, in the end, I no longer asked. I could not talk about it or about how I felt about it or, for that matter, how I felt about myself as a survivor. I didn't even know the word "survivor." When talking about friends we hadn't seen for a long time, the conversation would go something like this:

What happened to Mr. Levinsohn, Papi? And what happened to his dog?

Ah, Mr. Levinsohn, no, he didn't come back. We don't know what happened to him.

My parents would use the usual euphemism: *They didn't come back*, i.e., they were murdered, they didn't survive, they were murdered in some camp. When I met people in the street,

35

people I had known before the war, I automatically gave information, e.g. *Hello, Mrs. Cohn, how are you? My parents will be so happy that I have seen you*, meaning that my parents were alive, had survived. I never asked others what had happened to them or how their relatives were; after all I didn't know whether their relatives had come back. I only gave information and they would do the same. I then passed that on to my parents:

I met Mrs. Van der Beek today on my way home from school. She lives alone now. But her daughter lives in Den Haag.

My parents knew then that Mrs. Van der Beek's husband "had not come back." Family and friends had disappeared and were never seen again. Others emigrated shortly after the war to then Palestine (now Israel), to Australia or to the USA. I did not always get to say goodbye and in some cases never saw them again. In other cases, friends of the family might come back a few years later, after they had made a life for themselves in the new country, to visit us and other friends. It was then I would find out that, no, these friends were not, after all dead, as I had thought; they had emigrated and now came to see us.

A couple, Mr. and Mrs. Benjamin, had gone to the USA, lived in New York, and had made a new life for themselves. They came to visit a few years later and I was delighted; they had been among my favorite people.

Tante Jetty and Oom Fred, how wonderful to see you! Where have you been all this time? Have you come back to stay? No? Well, how long will you stay? How often will I see you? Where are you staying?

But even though we knew why Tante Jetty and Oom Fred had emigrated, nothing was ever said about the past, about anything that had happened to them. We simply ignored the subject; it was both an unwritten rule and an overt one. One of the things which were not talked about was Hans' family. Hans and I had been inseparable in Theresienstadt. He and his parents and older brother were deported in the fall transports of 1944. At that time, I only knew that these transports went to "the East." I also knew that that was a "bad place." I had not yet heard the name Auschwitz; I didn't yet know that people were gassed. After the war, silence reigned on this topic, at least in my family. Therefore I could no longer, after the first times, ask about Hans, could not ask whether anyone had seen his name on a survivors' list, could not ask what had happened to him or what my parents thought had happened to him. I simply assumed that he was dead, that the Nazis had murdered him. For all that assumption, though, I kept hoping that, some day, I would meet him on the street or at school or somewhere else.

There, that boy, he has light brown hair; could it be Hans? That other boy is small and slender; could it be? Maybe I will meet him at school? Surely they would have come back to Amsterdam, why can't I ever see him? Maybe he lives in another part of Amsterdam, Amsterdam-East? I wish I could ask somebody. But whom?

Even later, when I had grown up and had graduated from the lyceum, I still kept hoping that he had survived, a sort of hope against hope because I knew nothing. Still later, after I had emigrated to the United States, I was still having visions of seeing Hans somewhere, of instant recognition, of meeting again.

After all, if I could emigrate, then so could anyone else. Maybe his family has also come to the USA. Maybe he's the only one who survived and he came by himself. It could be possible, couldn't it? Others did, even children.

After my father died in 1980, I found in his papers a short note about a kibbutz in Israel, called Givat Chaim Ichud. They had (and still have) a museum about Theresienstadt as well as copies of the Theresienstadt records. I wrote to them in 1986 and asked if they had our name and the name of Hans' family in their records. Thus it was that not till 1986 did I find out that Hans and his family had been deported to Auschwitz and that they were gassed on arrival. After forty-one years of hope, this news came as a terrible shock—a physical shock, as though I had been hit in the stomach with a heavy stick—even though I had assumed his death all this time. But then: truth and assumption are two very different things. Perhaps if my parents and

I had been able to talk about this, the truth would have come out earlier and would not, therefore, have hit me so hard. However, we couldn't and my parents kept telling me:

You have to forget about all that now. It's past. It's over. You have to think of the future. You just go to school and do your school work, that is your job. Don't think about anything else, don't think about the past; don't talk about anything. The future is important.

The trouble was that I did not understand future.

How can I not think about what has happened? Can I force myself to forget? How do I do that? Thoughts just kind of come. How can I keep them away? Why do I have to? A future. What is a future? What does that mean? Why is it important? What do I do in the future? Is there even a future? What if the Nazis come back? Then I don't have a future, do I? How do you work for a future if you don't know what it is? How do you work for a future if you don't know that you'll have one? Does future mean next week? Next month? Next year? How can I think that far ahead?

I had just spent five years thinking only of the same day or maybe, possibly, the next day, certainly not of anything farther ahead. It made no sense to me—but I could not ask. Nor could I ask about other friends. My friend Max with whom I had been in first and second grade and who had disappeared one day, remained invisible after the war as well. Again I assumed that he had not survived. I had no idea where he had gone or what had become of him. Again, the truth came after forty-some years. Again, it came as a shock. This time, however, it was a good shock. On the first night of Chanukah in 1987, I got a phone call and it was Max! It was one of the best Chanukah presents I have ever had! It turned out that he and his parents had been hidden in a chicken coop for three years, together with two other adults. They had survived the war, though his father died shortly after. In 1946 he and his mother emigrated to the United States and, of course, if anybody in my family knew that, they did not tell me. So, as of 1987 we are in contact again, have visited back and forth and are, once again, or maybe still, friends.

Between the language changes and the silence, it was as though certain people had never existed. Because of having to remain silent myself, it was as if I did not exist.

Gabriele at age seven, December 1940, second grade.

Max at age seven, December 1940, second grade.

Max and Gabriele in California, around 1990,
approximately aged fifty-seven.

⟋ *Elementary School*

In August of that year, 1945, Elementary School started again, after the summer vacation was over. I had thought that my mother would take me that first day, but that was not to be.

You are old enough to go by yourself. Just go to school, you know where it is. When you get there, go find Mijnheer Zandvoort, Mr. Zandvoort. He is the principal and he will take you to your class.

I was frightened out of my wits; I knew where the school was but had never met, or even seen, Mr. Zandvoort. How was I to find him?

I can't just go and "find" him; how do I do that? I don't even know where to ask for him! Does he have a classroom? If he doesn't, what do I do? The school has two parts; in which part do I look for him? And what do I do if I don't find him at all?

But, I had to go and so I went. I not only did not know Mr. Zandvoort; I had no books, no paper, no pencils and no pen. At that time we still wrote sometimes on a *lei*, a slate. To do that, one needed a *griffel*, a slate-pencil. These were kept in a *griffel-doos*, a special box, made of wood, with a sliding cover, often decorated. It also held a small sponge and a small chamois, both used to clean the slate. I had no slate, no *griffel* and, for sure, no *griffeldoos*. I had nothing. As a result, I was not only afraid, I was ashamed. It was another flaw in me. In the event, I did find Mr.

43

Zandvoort, by asking the first person I saw whether he was Mr. Zandvoort, and, lo and behold, he was. He took me to my class-room and introduced me to my teacher, Mijnheer Hogedoorn, Mr. Hogedoorn, who assigned me a seat, somewhere in the middle of a row, next to another girl. I didn't know anyone in that class, naturally. They, instead, had been together as a class since fourth grade. So I didn't fit in. Mr. Hogedoorn looked very big to me and very stern. There were boys in that class who looked very big and tall. I was twelve years old, and knew I should have been at least in sixth grade, if not already in seventh. But these boys looked older than I was. I felt very small and very ashamed: not only did I not have any of the necessary things, I did not know anything much. The last grade I had been in had been second grade. I had no idea what to expect or what might have been taught in the grades I had missed.

Why does Mr. Hogedoorn look so stern? And why are those boys so old? They don't really belong in fifth grade. In fact, I don't belong here; I don't know anything and they will laugh at me, I know they will.

In actual fact, the "older" boys were older; they had also been in concentration camps, or in hiding or at forced labor. They had missed as much school as I had, only I didn't know it yet. As for the sternness of Mr. Hogedoorn, he certainly needed it to deal with those sixteen-year-old boys who didn't want to be in the same grade with us babies and who yet could not go to a higher grade.

On various occasions, things came up which I had never heard about; when I asked what something meant, my worst fear came true because the others did laugh at me. Mr. Hogedoorn, however, did not let that go by; he immediately told them not to laugh at anybody; we, who were so much behind, could not help our being behind and we would catch up soon enough. He taught them not to be biased or prejudiced. As for catching up, I tried hard to catch up, but it was hard work and I had trouble concentrating as well as trouble learning the material. I also had trouble understanding why I had to learn it; I didn't know what it was good for. I only knew that, once again, I had to do what I was told. Was that the freedom everyone talked about?

I also had trouble getting to know the other children. I didn't know how to go about that, I had no idea of what to say, how to get to know anybody. I did not know how to play. In the camps I had forgotten what "play" meant; I had now no idea what to do. So I ended up being somewhat of a loner. My best friends were books; they opened another world for me. They showed me a world I had never heard about, not necessarily a real world, but at least a world I could understand and which was real to me. I read whatever I could get my hands on: one of the authors was Karl May who wrote (without ever having been there) about the American West, about Native Americans and their relationships with Whites. There were sympathetic characters, there were animals, there were fast horses and many adventures and I loved it all. I read a lot of fairy tales, Hans Christian Anderson, the brothers Grimm and others. My father bought me a lot of books about discoveries: C.W. Ceram and others about archeology; books about medical discoveries. I read anything and everything in my parents' bookcase; I had permission to read anything I wanted. My parents had the point of view that if I understood it, I might as well read it, and if I did not understand, then it couldn't do me any harm because I would probably skip the parts I didn't understand. And so it was. I read about the Armenian genocide: *The Forty Days of the Musa Dagh*; and, much later in High School, I read Charles Dickens, Hemingway, Goethe, Schiller and various French authors—these were school assignments but I loved them nevertheless. So I had no trouble with reading. While still in Elementary School, my parents gave me a book about Amsterdam's airport: Schiphol. It was mostly a description of various jobs and taught me how airplanes fly. I was fascinated and on one occasion held forth to my mother for over three hours, telling her everything I had learned—and, undoubtedly, far more than she ever wanted to know about the subject!

Twice in my life, my mother told me about certain books:
I don't think you'd be interested in that.

To this day, I have not read those books.

My main trouble at school was arithmetic. I had not learned
fractions or percentages; I barely knew how to do long divisions
and how to do subtractions. Even today, so many years later, I
have not caught up; subtractions are still difficult, I still don't
know fractions and know percentages only very vaguely. Luck-
ily, today we have calculators which can do all those things perfectly! My secondary trouble at school was children who teased
me. I had no idea what teasing was and took everything seriously. That got me into a number of fights. Then also, there were
children who came from what the Dutch then called *foute
ouders*, literally "wrong parents," i.e. parents who had sided
with the Nazis and may have been members of the N.S.B., the
Nationaal Socialistische Bond, the Dutch Nazi party, or, if not
members, then at least sympathizers and, possibly, helpers.
Those children called us "Dirty Jews" and other such names.
When Mr. Hogedoorn found out about it (from others, never
from us Jewish children), he would not only punish the others,
but also tell them why they shouldn't say such things. But I got
into a number of fights with those children as well; the only
thing I knew to do when they called me names or cursed me out
was to slap their faces. They did not take that, needless to say,
and so there were any number of fights.

Outside of school I mostly kept to myself. I stayed inside
myself; it was the easiest way. I could not talk about the recent
past, nobody wanted to hear what I thought and the very few
times when someone spoke about it and I said something, I
heard:

*Oh, you were only a child, you can't possibly know. You were only
a child, you couldn't have suffered. You were only a child, you didn't
understand.* Or even: *That can't be right, you're only a child, you
cannot possibly remember.*

I learned very quickly to keep my mouth firmly shut. In a
way, I lost myself; I shut the past away into a drawer, locked it

tightly, and then threw the key away. On the cattle car ride from Amsterdam to Westerbork, I had essentially gone "numb." I no longer felt anything, I no longer cared, I no longer cried, I had no tears. That numbness remained with me after the war and for many, many years after. It meant that I didn't feel any joy, but also that I didn't feel any pain. It kept memories in check so that they could not come forward and bother or frighten me. I did not feel fear. It came in handy in Elementary School when, once again, I didn't know an answer or when, once again, I didn't understand what Mijnheer Hogedoorn was talking about, or when, once again, I couldn't see where a certain city was located on the map, or when, once again, others called me names. I fought, yes, but not because it made me feel bad. It didn't make me feel anything; I just knew that they shouldn't be allowed to say such things. Just because I was unable to feel anything did not mean that they could do or say whatever they wanted. I felt nothing. To me, I didn't exist. How can you exist when you don't feel anything? Do you really exist when you don't say anything? If you have to keep quiet, do you then really exist?

Two other things happened in Elementary School which were very disturbing to me: my mother took me to the dentist and I had to get braces for my overbite. At that time they didn't look the way they do now: there was a main part which fit exactly into the roof of my mouth and another part which was the wire that went in front of my teeth. The main part came in two halves, connected by a small screw. As the case might be, the wire was tightened or loosened by turning the screw to make the two halves go closer together or farther apart. The braces were not only painful, but they made me lisp. I hated them from the day I got them. Unfortunately for me, I had to wear them until I was about nineteen years old, a very long time, especially for a child who already thought of herself as ugly.

The other thing happened while we were still with Carla's family. Long ago I wrote a story about this event, which follows here:

Discovery

The teacher stood in front of the board with his long wooden pointer. "Which river is this, Pom?" As usual, Pom knew the answer and the teacher smiled and asked the next student: "What is the main island of Zeeland, Nicholas?" The boy hesitated, then answered the question. The teacher pointed to cities, rivers, provinces and the students named them. A typical geography lesson in fifth grade. I had studied hard for this one. For hours I had pored over my school atlas, memorizing the spelling of the unfamiliar names, trying to locate the little red dots which were cities. For most of the other students this was repetition, but I had missed third and fourth grade because of the war, and geography, as well as a number of other things, was new to me. The big map of Holland which hung in front of the class didn't seem to represent anything. Fat black lines, thin black lines, red squares, red dots and blue shapes—what did it all mean? When I stood near the map, everything was out of proportion and when I was in my seat the map showed shapes which in no way resembled the pages in my atlas. My school atlas had one map for each province, but the big map showed the whole country. Cities which were far apart in my atlas were near each other on the big map. Whenever the teacher asked me a question, I had to go through a long process of deciding that this city must be in such a province and therefore had to be Eindhoven. At the end of the process I usually gave a wrong answer. It wasn't long before the geography hour had become one of the many hours of pure torture. I studied harder, my father would show me places on the "blind" map—the map without names—and I would point out cities, rivers and territories. But when the wooden rod, like an extension of the teacher's finger, moved from dot to dot, I could no longer relate to them and had to sit silently, crying inside.

One day again, the teacher showed me a city and asked me the name, and, as usual, I said the wrong name. But this time the teacher said: "No, that isn't right, it's in Limburg, not in

Brabant." I was surprised for there was no separation between the provinces. On my way home that day, I admired the trees in the street with their solid green tops and wondered that the heavy tops didn't pull the trees down. Someone came up to me saying hello and asking whether I had not seen him wave at me. He never gave me a chance to answer, though, but told me to say hello to my parents for him. At home I talked my geography problems over with Carla, my childhood friend who lived in the apartment above ours before the war. At this time, though, my family was living with hers because, coming out of the concentration camp, we had no other place to go. For seven people the small apartment was rather crowded but for me it was almost like having two sisters: Carla, and the elder girl, Willy. Neither of them had any suggestions to offer for my problem, however, so I sighed and studied some more, but to no avail.

One Sunday Carla was playing the piano while Willy and I stood near and watched. At the other end of the suite, formed by the dining room where the piano stood and the living room, sat the four parents, drinking tea and discussing something. Suddenly my father called out to us and held something up in the air while he said: "Do you want it?" I looked at him and asked: "What is it?" He just repeated the original question: "Do you want it?" So I said again: "What is it?" "*Do you want it?*" "*What is it?*"

My father must have realized that I was serious. He got up and came toward me, still holding the object, asking me again whether I wanted it. By the time he had crossed the whole living room, I saw what he held. It was one of those square, dry cookies which we occasionally had with our tea whenever our rationing card allowed such luxuries.

Two days later my mother and I were in the doctor's office where I had to look at things. As soon as he picked up his pointer, I was afraid. He pointed to a space and asked me: "Is this first sign a triangle or a circle?" "Where is the sign?" I asked in my turn. He didn't answer but instead said: "Look at the card and tell me the name of the first letter you see." "What card?" was

my answer. He just shook his head and put some sort of con-
struction in front of my eyes, placed some lenses in it and, lo
and behold, there *was* a card! This time I read the first letter
without hesitation. A few weeks after that, I owned my first pair
of glasses and discovered the world. I found out why the tree-
tops didn't pull the trees down—they weren't solid! They had
leaves, thousands of them, and between the leaves, I found,
were birds, hopping around on branches. My parents' friends
no longer asked whether I hadn't seen them waving at me and it
turned out that the shadows on the other side of the street
weren't shadows at all, but people just like me. The small blurs I
had so often wondered about, I now identified as dogs and the
colored carpet in the street turned out to be grass with flowers.
Even the big map in front of the classroom was endowed with
provinces and black borderlines between them. And the blue
shapes, I now discovered, were lakes. Every morning I would
put on my round, metal-framed glasses and every day my
friends would tease me that I looked like an owl. But suddenly
bicycle riding became fun; even just walking through the streets
was fun, because now I could look at everything and really enjoy it because all of a sudden I could see.

I wore my glassses, yes, and I could see, yes, but I hated them
almost as much as the braces because I thought they looked
ugly and made me look ugly and not being able to see was yet
another flaw in me. They did have one advantage, though.
They made me see the world around me as it really was, not as I
had thought it was.

⌒ *Manners*

Several people took me in hand and taught me manners—manners which I had, of course, been taught before the war, but which I had forgotten in the camps. Concentration camp life does not make for good manners! One of those occasions which has remained with me was a day shortly after Elementary School had started. Carla, by now, was two years ahead of me and therefore in what would be seventh grade here in the USA. She needed something for school and I needed some ink, probably also for school or at least for school work. So we went off together to the local stationer's shop, called De Roode, and she bought whatever it was she needed. Then it was my turn. I looked at the salesman and said:

A bottle of ink.

He gave it to me, I paid and we walked out. When we were on the way home, Carla said to me:

You know, you should have said: "A bottle of ink, please." Or maybe: "May I have a bottle of ink?" Then, after, you should have said: "Thank you."

Carla was almost twelve then; I was already twelve. I don't remember what I answered, but I've been grateful for that lesson ever since. I also remember that I never again went into a store without saying "please" and "thank you." But on that day,

I was ashamed again and thought that not saying *Please* or *Thank you* and not asking politely was one more flaw in me. It seemed to me that I was going from bad to worse.

My mother, naturally, took me in hand for everyday manners, for when to say "please" and "thank you," when to ask questions, how to ask questions, when to be silent. She taught me, again, to answer politely when adults spoke to me. She taught me, again, to—as they say in Holland—"speak with two words," i.e., I was not to say just "yes" or "no," but instead "yes, Mrs. Trap" or "no, Mr. Groen," or the equivalent of the English: "Yes, Sir" or "No, Ma'am." She taught me, again, to use the polite form, rather than the familiar form. The Dutch language has both and using the wrong form can be insulting, even very insulting. I knew all this very well before the war, but in the first three years of the war and later, in the concentration camps, these ideas had disappeared. They had no survival value and consequently we children forgot about them and became little savages who had to be taught all this all over again. No one in the camps had said "please" or "thank you"; no one had said: "Yes, Sir" or "No, Ma'am"; at best people had pushed me out of the way. Since I had dealt mostly with other camp children, I had no use for polite forms. Anything which had nothing to do with survival, went out of our heads—or at least out of mine. Now I had to start all over again. I had, also, to unlearn a good many things of which stealing was but one. In the camp, when I saw some food which was not well guarded, I stole it and ate it. After I had eaten it, nobody could steal it from me. It meant one more day of life. Now, after the war, after we had returned to Amsterdam, those habits had to be unlearned and changed. It was no longer all right to steal food or to take some from the kitchen without asking, and asking politely. It was no longer all right to take anything without asking and asking politely.

My mother also taught me not to complain about anything. Instead I should just keep a smile on my face; other people would not be interested in my little woes or complaints and it was impolite to mention those things. She re-taught me table manners. Before the war, after my grandmother had moved in with us, she was the one who had taught me which fork and knife to use and to use the bigger size. For lunch, in those days, we used silverware of a smaller size, for dinner we used the bigger size. Up to that time, my parents had allowed me to use the smaller size even for dinner since I was small for my age and therefore had small hands. My grandmother would not stand for that at all and taught me to handle the bigger ones. After the war, my mother had to re-teach me, since I had long forgotten this kind of thing. Again, just as the concentration camp was no place for manners, it equally was no place for the "correct" silverware. We were happy if we *had* a fork or spoon. My mother also taught me how to set the table. True, I couldn't carry very much at one time, but I could and did make several trips from the kitchen to the dining room to put the plates on the table and then also the knives, forks, and spoons. Putting them on the table was no problem, but I had to learn also just where they went.

Then there was the problem of what to say when I met someone new or saw someone whom I already knew. I had to greet these people and to ask how they were and how their husbands or wives were (if any) and, of course, I was to ask after the children, if they had any. Just as I provided information to my parents' friends so that they wouldn't have to ask about my parents, they also provided information to us. Someone might say:

My husband badly wants to talk to your husband; when will he be home?

This assumed of course that the lady asking this already knew that my father had come back from the camps. Or, if another lady saw my mother and me together, she might invite me to come and play with her children, thereby giving us the information that her children were alive and healthy. If they were not healthy, they couldn't play. So conversations were rather roundabout. It was, actually, a sort of code.

My parents, and in particular my mother, were very insistent that I should know and use good manners. Later, much later, when we had, once again, a telephone, I was taught how to answer it and also what to say if I made a call. In answering, I had to use, not the family name, but the firm name. My father had his office at home and most phone calls were, therefore, for the office. In initiating a call, I had to greet the person on the other side, then ask to speak, please, to whoever it was. At all times, I had to be polite.

I was in my teens by then and so I rather minded this incessant harping (in my opinion) on manners. I did not have a "rebellious age" as such; that didn't come till very much later, but I resented being told what to do. But then...at that age I resented most everything, especially authority. Still, I didn't say anything about it and just resented in silence. As far as I could see, my parents had had and still had enough trouble and did not need any more from me. I was determined not to make more trouble for them. My actual "rebellious age" didn't happen until I was twenty and over. Even then, the rebellion was very minor.

Eventually, when I was about eighteen, my parents started teaching me how to behave when we went out to eat in a restaurant. Actually, before that, there were not many restaurants open in Amsterdam. My parents, once we had a little more money, went to those which were open and they had always taken me along. But as of age seventeen or eighteen, I got proper lessons in behavior when we ate out. This included reading a menu, being polite to the waiters, what wine to choose with the meal and out of which glass to drink it. I have to say that this didn't stay with me very well and that, in any event, times have changed and are less formal now than they were then.

Why was all this so important? Well, if I knew how to behave, then I would not attract attention. As a Jew, to attract attention was, to my parents and particularly to my father, one of the worst things which could happen. To attract attention was to stand out, to make people notice you. After the war and after the camps, being noticed was the last thing anybody wanted. Therefore, we dressed conservatively, we used the appropriate manners, we tried to fit in any way we could. The problem was, we never really did fit in—or, at least, I didn't think I did. In spite of the good manners and all that goes with them, I was not like other teenagers. Granted, I was moody and in turn happy and sullen, as teenagers tend to be, but I was not carefree (whether that was a mood put on or true), I did not chatter on the phone, I did not giggle and, in fact, rarely laughed. My parents were very introverted and, I suppose in minor part by imitation and in major part because of the "numbness," I became so too. I don't remember how my parents were before the war, but from what cousins of theirs have told me, my mother was fun loving and liked to go out, dance and laugh. My father liked fun, but was more introverted than my mother. After the war, my mother never, ever laughed aloud again; she just smiled occasionally. Both of them were far more introverted after the war than before. None of us could speak about what had happened and so it all just became hidden in our minds and souls. It was pushed away in the hope that it would never come out again. I do not know how my parents eventually dealt with that; they never spoke about anything to do with the war and the camps to me and I knew better than to ask questions. This has stayed with me; I still do not ask questions, even if I know people quite well.

☞ *Denmark*

While I was still in fifth grade, in the fall of 1945, an invitation came from my uncle in Denmark. Transports of Dutch children had started to go to Denmark, by invitation of the Danes. Our Dutch children were so starved that they resembled little old people, skin and bones, wrinkles and huge eyes. The Danes had invited the Dutch children to come to Denmark, to be hosted by a Danish family for three months in order to put some flesh and muscle on their bones. We went, in other words, to be fattened up. My Uncle Hans had invited me. In actual fact he was not my uncle; he was my father's first cousin, his mother was a sister of my paternal grandmother. He was a few years older than my father and I was told to call him Uncle Hans. He had married a Danish girl before the war and had gone to live in Denmark with her. They had a son, but after a few years they divorced, yet my uncle stayed in Denmark. When, during the war, the Nazis wanted to deport the Jews to concentration camps as they had done and were doing in other countries, a warning went out to the Jewish population. All were told to go to the seashore. They did and from there, Danish fishermen and other boat owners took them to neutral Sweden. Sweden received them and they were able to stay in Sweden until the war was over. Of the thousands of Danish Jews, only about

300—who had not received the warning in time—were sent to Theresienstadt. With the exception of one or two people, they all survived and were taken back home by the Swedish Red Cross during the last days of the war.

When I first heard about Uncle Hans, he had been divorced for a while and had a second wife. I was to stay with him and his wife. They lived in Charlottenlund, a suburb of Copenhagen, where they had a big house. Or at least it seemed very big to me. I did not know my Uncle Hans or any of his family. The invitation scared me, I did not want to be separated from my parents, I did not want to leave our familiar apartment, I did not want to leave Amsterdam again, I did not want to leave Holland again, and I did not want to leave school which was by now familiar and where I at least knew the teacher and my classmates. I did not want to miss three more months, after all I had already missed. I had not caught up to where I should be; three months seemed a very long time to go away, to a family I had never heard about and did not know. But all my begging and pleading was of no use whatsoever; I had not been asked whether I wanted to go. My parents said that I had to go and so preparations were made and I went. In 2001 I wrote a poem about this not very good experience. I shall quote it here.

DENMARK

We emerged, my parents and I,
half-starved, emaciated, weak,
but alive and together,
from the concentration camps
in June nineteen forty-five.

Came August
and school started.
I was placed in fifth grade
even though I had missed
third and fourth.
But...at age twelve
I was too old
for third grade.

Regrettably,
I did not understand
much of what we learned.
I was a misfit
and, therefore, unhappy.

In October or November
a letter arrived
from my uncle in Denmark,
inviting me
to stay with him
for three months.

I did not want to go,
had no mind
to leave my parents;
separation, in my experience,
had too often proven
to be permanent.

I went with one
of many children's transports,
then going from Holland
to Denmark
where we children would be able
to eat our fill
and gain much needed weight.

* * *

I am on a train,
a card on a string
around my neck,
stating my name
and other details.
There are many other children,
most crying for their mothers.
The accompanying adults
don't quite know
what to do with us.

We are too thin,
our clothes are shabby
and don't fit us well;
we don't want to eat
the food we are given;
we want our Mami.

I am silent,
not crying,
not laughing,
not speaking,
a misfit again,
and, therefore, unhappy.

Somebody hands us
a booklet with Danish phrases.
Nobody knows
how to pronounce these words,
so we use Dutch pronunciation.
When the train finally arrives,
our foster families
cannot understand us,
nor we them,
and we don't know
what will happen next.

I go home with my uncle
whom I have never met before
but who speaks German as I do,
so we understand each other.
His wife is Danish
and speaks only Danish.
I cannot communicate with her.
I feel that I don't belong here,
I don't fit in;
I am unhappy.

I am sent to school,
a Danish school of course,
and, once again,
I do not grasp
what I am supposed to learn.
I don't belong here.
I am, once again, a misfit
and, therefore, unhappy.
My uncle, who is kind
and who means well,
has no idea what to do
with a severely damaged child.
I am silent most of the time.
He cannot fathom
why I don't talk as other children do.

Every Sunday
we go for a walk
into the woods:
my uncle, my aunt,
the dog and I.
I do not run
or play with the dog.
I do not talk to him either.

I walk sedately
together with my uncle and aunt
because I don't know
what else to do:
I don't know if I'm allowed to run
and, if I'm not allowed,
then what will happen?

For Christmas that year,
they give me
a paper doll
with paper clothes
to cut out and dress her in.
I have no idea
what to do with this doll
or with her clothes.
My aunt has to show me.
I don't talk to the doll;
my uncle asks me:
"Why don't you talk to her?"

I just look at him.
How would I know
what to say?
He doesn't realize
that I no longer know
how to play,
that I don't understand
what my uncle means.

* * *

After three months
I went home again.
This visit was not a success:
I gained no weight,
learned very little Danish
and very little else
in the Danish school.

What I did learn is
that I want to stay home
with my parents,
in Holland
where I belong
even if I don't know
the answers in
my fifth grade class.
But here, with my people,
I mostly belong;
I may not be completely happy,
but I'm no longer so unhappy.

My uncle had had the same upbringing as my parents and as such knew that he was Jewish, but did not practice Judaism. Like my parents he tried to fit in and, amongst other things, that meant having a Christmas tree and celebrating Christmas in some way, even if only by giving gifts. At home, we also had a Christmas tree and gave gifts, but my mother also lit the candles in the *Chanukiah* or, as it is also called, the *Chanukah menorah*. This is an eight-branched candelabra into which candles are placed. There is also a single candle, a little aside or up higher possibly. This last one is called the *shamash* or "servant" (literally: one who serves) and the other lights are lit with it, never with a match. But on Chanukah people also give gifts, so I saw no difference at that time between the two festivals. I had learned nothing about either one; my parents were, after all, assimilated and had not told me about Chanukah; on the other hand, I doubt that they knew very much about Christmas.

My Uncle Hans sent me to the local school where, first of all, I had trouble with the language. Of course I did not speak Danish and, equally of course, teaching was done in Danish. In the school most students were, of course, Danes, but there were also three Dutch boys who had also come on one of these children's transports. The oldest was called Henk; he had red hair. The middle one was called Karel; he had dark hair. The youngest was my age, twelve, and was called Jo. Jo and I had problems from the beginning. He was a war-wild child as much as I was and neither of us was inclined to "take" anything from the other. Generally we did not actually fight, except for once when Jo decided that he was going to show me his new knife. This he did by cutting me across the hand whereupon I slapped his face. In no time we were rolling on the floor, in a fight, until the teacher came and hauled both of us up. I no longer remember whether either or both of us were punished. Henk must have been about fifteen by then and more or less took responsibility for the rest of us. What he did for Karel and Jo, I don't know, but he helped me understand the teacher, explained what I had not understood, talked to me about Holland and his family and generally became a friend, even though he was fifteen and I was only twelve. Long after we returned to Holland we kept up the contact through letters—he lived in Utrecht—and occasional visits. I must have been about seventeen when Henk was, once again, in Amsterdam. On this occasion he had asked me beforehand, by letter, if I would go out with him, to the movies. I had said yes, but when he arrived and the evening came, I was afraid.

What do I say? How do I behave? What if he wants to hold my hand? Or if my friends see us? What will they think? What do I think? I'm scared. I've never gone to the movies with a boy. Maybe he wants to kiss me. Should I allow that? What would happen if I do? No, I can't do that, it would be awful! This is terrible—I don't know what to do.

In the end I went with him to the movies, of course, and as it turned out, we were still just friends; he didn't hold my hand or kiss me and all was well. After the movie, he took me home and we parted as we had met, friends but not boyfriend and girlfriend.

My uncle and I also had some problems. He did not really understand children, did not know how to talk to them or to play with them. He had a son of his own, but Erik was grown and no longer lived with the family. One day, he came to visit. I had not met him before and was very impressed by him; he was about ten years older than I and therefore grown up. After a while, he took me outside into the garden and taught me to play ball. He threw the ball (where it came from, I do not know, I no longer remember) to me and I caught it and then threw it back. He had to teach me, though, because I did not remember ever having played ball. Eventually we threw the ball against the wall of the house; I tried to throw it as high as my grown-up cousin did. Of course I did not succeed, but for once I did not mind. Then came disaster! My cousin threw the ball with a fair amount of force. It should have gone against the wall but instead it went against—and of course through—the window. The window was closed at the time! We heard the sound of

breaking glass and waited. Sure enough, my uncle came storm-
ing out of the door, absolutely furious. I immediately ducked,
even though it did not look as though my uncle was going to hit
either one of us—but mine was an early-learned reaction. I also
immediately assumed that I would be held guilty; after all, I was
the younger one and supposedly children play, therefore, since
I was a child, I had played and this was the result. To my great
surprise, nothing happened to me because my cousin immediately told my uncle that he was the one who had thrown the
ball. My uncle muttered a remark about grown-ups not being
so childish as to play with balls and I suppose, in hindsight, that
he made my cousin pay for the window. I thought then and still
think now that it was truly kind of a twenty-two-year-old to
take an interest in a twelve-year-old and try to amuse her. He
was very sweet to me and I have never forgotten. Unfortunately, I never saw him again; he did not again come to the house
and, after I returned to Holland, there was no opportunity to
meet him again. Both before my cousin's visit and after, I felt
lonely and very alone. Once again I did not fit in, neither at my
uncle's house nor at school. My uncle went to work every day
and I could not talk to the rest of the family, so I was on my own,
except on school days. On Sundays, my uncle was there but we
didn't talk very much together. He probably did not know how
to talk to me any more than I knew how to talk to him. And the
old taboos held. Children are seen but not heard, don't take
part in grown-ups' conversations, don't ask questions, and so
on. I certainly could not talk about the war with him and even
less about the camps.

My uncle made me do various jobs, in and around the
house, for example bring in the pail with coal for heating, which
I resented no end. It reminded me of the work I had had to do in
Theresienstadt but I could not tell him that since I could not
talk to him about that time at all. My uncle and aunt were very
good to me, they bought me clothes and a warm coat, they gave
me presents for Christmas and they fed me a lot of food. I was
grateful but remained lonely and alone. Gratefulness is not

Right:
My mother
and father,
New Year's Eve
1950–1951.

Below:
My father
and mother,
1954.

*My mother, Ilse,
and her sister, Ulle
(Ursula), 1951.*

Ulle, 1973.

necessarily a pleasant feeling, especially when it feels like charity, and it doesn't alleviate loneliness.

Finally the three months had passed and I went home, again by train, though I have no recollection of that trip. When the train arrived at the Central Station, the smallest children had forgotten their Dutch and now spoke only Danish. We older children had to translate for the parents who were, naturally, most upset. I had not learned much Danish, since my uncle spoke German and the Dutch boys spoke Dutch. Today I remember none of it. I was happy to be home, to be reunited with my parents, to go back to our apartment and to have my room back. All the familiar things were still there and I thought that I could finally settle down.

◠ Het Amsterdams Lyceum

After my return from Denmark, my parents arranged tutoring for me by Mijnheer Hogedoorn. I was supposed to catch up with my fifth grade. The tutoring helped, that is true, but I never did catch up completely. Throughout the remainder of fifth grade and, later, sixth grade, there were always things I did not know and could not understand. In addition, I had trouble concentrating and, at any time, would rather read a book than do my homework. But even when I did my homework, I was easily sidetracked. I didn't really see the relevance of school in general and of what I was learning. At that time, the Dutch language was still inflected, much like Latin and German, and I had to learn these inflections. A new spelling had just been introduced and we had to learn that as well. I didn't see what possible difference it could make how I spelled a word or, more in particular, how I used one word ending as opposed to another. Soon thereafter the declensions were no longer used and the language was therefore simpler. While I was still struggling in sixth grade, my father decided that I should go to a lyceum afterwards, the Amsterdams Lyceum, which was quite well-known. The Dutch school system, at that time, was quite different from the American one: Elementary School consisted of six grades, starting at age six, after which came High School from

71

seventh grade through twelfth grade. Some of that has changed
again since my High School graduation. A lyceum had two divisions to it: a modern division and a classical division where we
learned Latin and Greek, as well as three Foreign Languages.
In the modern division, only the three Foreign Languages were
taught: English, French, and German. Both divisions also had
an A section and a B section. In the A section, more language
was taught; in the B section, the emphasis was on mathematics.
We had no choice of classes, either. The program was set and all
we had to do was to follow it.

Some time during my sixth grade year, I was sent to the
Amsterdams Lyceum to take an entrance exam. It frightened
me even before I went because I had no idea what would be
asked and nobody explained anything. I no longer remember
all the parts of this entrance exam, but I do remember the arithmetic part. We were to add the numbers given to us and then
write only the last number of the answer in the space provided.
Since I was very bad in arithmetic, this scared me badly. But I
had to do it and so I did. To this day, I have no idea how well or
how badly I did on that test, but in any event I was accepted at
the lyceum. So in September of 1947, at the age of fourteen, I
began school at the Amsterdams Lyceum. The first two years
were identical for everyone, thereafter came the division between classical and modern. Once again, we learned Dutch
grammar and once again I did not understand. I had no concep-
tion of any grammatical terms, had no idea of the difference
between a noun and an adjective and had never parsed a sentence. But we also had to write compositions every week and,
for some reason, I was good at those. Sometimes the theme was
set, other times we had what we called a "free" composition,
i.e., we could choose the subject. In the second or third year of
my lyceum time, I began to write about my war experiences but
having had the experience that nobody wanted to hear about it
and that, in any event, I was "only" a child, I wrote in the third
person instead of the first. I wrote about "the girl" or "a girl and
a boy," without names. I thought that that would make it more

like fiction and therefore maybe more acceptable. One time I wrote a composition entitled "The Different One." The main character was a girl who happened to be Jewish and what happened to her during the war. It spoke of the yellow star we had to wear, of the fear of the unknown and the fear of the "bad places." When I got it back, the teacher had written on it: "That isn't all that different!" I took the hint and wrote no more about such things. It was obvious that nobody wanted to hear about it, even several years after the war and even in fictional form. So the silence continued.

We were taught ancient history and mythology and I loved both. I also loved history. The people in mythology—and the gods and heroes—were real to me; I could identify with them. I could understand what they did and why they did it. The historical people, both of ancient and modern history, were interesting; they had had adventures and they had presence. We also began mathematics: both algebra and geometry. To say that I did not understand either of these, is an understatement. Where I could at least vaguely see the use of geometry, I never did understand why it was necessary to add a to b, to find a result that was yet another letter. It meant less than nothing. Because of this I did badly and, once again, had to have tutoring. Thanks to the goodness of heart of my teacher and the help of my tutor, I managed to pass the first two years. Meanwhile I was missing a lot, once again, because I was often ill. Probably as a result of the war and camp years, I got every illness which came around plus a few others. The first year I had to have my tonsils out; the next year I had an appendectomy. I had at least one flu every year as well as numerous colds and ear infections and very often a fever without other symptoms. That didn't make for continuity in my studies. When I was fifteen, I came down with what is now known as rheumatoid arthritis. That limited me somewhat but not a lot since, in the beginning, it was not too bad. The only thing that really disturbed me about it was that it made me different again from the other students. There were certain things, like physical education classes, in

which I was not allowed to participate. The doctor also told me
to keep warm; therefore from that day on, I wore long pants
which was, at that time, most unusual. In fact, my parents had
to ask the school for permission so that I could wear pants.
Once again, I was different; once again I didn't fit in.

Some time during those first two years, it began to occur to
me that maybe there was something useful in school after all.
I had no specific plans for the future, I was still not at all sure
that I even *had* a future, but slowly off and on I thought of a profession. Actually that wasn't too difficult. From the time I was
eight years old I had always said that I wanted to become either
a pharmacist or an author. But even in the lyceum I had no idea
how to go about that. I was still just going to school because I
had to. I was still looking at just one day at a time or maybe a
very short time ahead. It was a sort of "automatic" living where
one day followed another but they were sort of empty. Before
and after school, I studied; other than that, I did not fill my days
with any prepared plans. I just *was*. I had no long-term plans
and did not know how to make any. How do you make long-
term plans if you're not sure of having a future? Even though I
was still saying that I wanted to be a pharmacist or an author,
I had not even the vaguest idea what that would entail or how I
would get there.

After these first two lyceum years, I had it more firmly in
mind, finally, to become a pharmacist, like my father. For that
path of study, the classical division of the lyceum was required.
So in my third lyceum year I started Greek and Latin as well as
various other new subjects. And, of course, the expected did
happen: I did not understand Latin at all. Its declensions, inflections and conjugations had nothing in common with what I
had earlier learned, not even anything with the Dutch inflections (which by then were no longer being used). It was beyond
me. So I learned by heart what I could, but was never able to
actually understand what I was doing. Greek, for some reason,
was considerably easier. But there were also botany and zoology and, as with algebra, I saw no reason to learn how plants

were put together. As for zoology, I liked it but had trouble with it, as with everything else. The fact that I could not understand what I was doing led me to the automatic conclusion that this was one more flaw in me. The teacher said, after all, that we were to study this picture or that page and everyone else managed. I didn't, so therefore I was stupid. I figured that was just one more flaw because of being Jewish. One flaw pulls another one after it: being Jewish caused all the other flaws.

Eventually I changed my mind about being a pharmacist and changed over to the modern division of the lyceum. Surprisingly, at least to me, it turned out that I was good, in fact very good, at modern languages. For the first time in my school life, I began to get good grades. English was no problem at all; it even was fun after a while. German I spoke at home and all I had to do was to learn some rules by heart. Also no problem. French was more difficult. In the beginning most of what we learned were verb conjugations in all possible and impossible tenses and moods. We also translated a lot. Then came summer vacation and my mother took me to Aix-Les-Bains in France. Aix was known for its curative waters for arthritis and that was the reason we went there. While the sojourn there didn't do anything for my arthritis, my mother, to her horror, found out that, after a year or two of French, I could not cobble a whole sentence together. So she sent me out on errands, to buy postcards, or things of that type. What she didn't know was that I would enter the shop, look around carefully, then point to the cards and say: "Ça, s'il vous plaît," "That, please." Obviously, that worked, but it hardly taught me to speak French. On our return to Amsterdam, my mother found me a conversation teacher, a French lady, Madame Matthieu, who taught French conversation to earn her living. The first time my mother took me to Madame Matthieu, Madame asked me to name the objects in the room: a table, a chair, etc. I couldn't do it. From then on, I had to go once a week and every week I had to write a composition for Madame and she corrected it as I sat there and explained why something was wrong. Then we would speak

French for an hour. And, after a couple of weeks, I found out that I could actually *use* this language for something. I could communicate. Not fluently, not correctly, but still, Madame understood what I said and I got an answer that fitted my question or statement. From that moment on, French became fun. My French teacher in the lyceum, Mijnheer Van Praag, had a habit of combining the words from two or three sentences and making us translate his made-up sentence from Dutch to French. And, all of a sudden, I realized what he was doing and studied differently and when he called on me (we had to come to the front of the class!), I was able to translate whatever he said. It amazed him, it amazed the whole class and, most of all, it amazed me. It made me feel that I was, after all, able to do the work. That, maybe, I was even a little less stupid than I had thought.

So my lyceum years passed. In the last grade we began to study for our final exams, the school exit exams. The final exam was the same everywhere in Holland for every same level of various schools. It was a state exam. It went over the last three years of study and over all of the fifteen or so subjects which we had studied. If we passed the written part, we were then allowed to study for the oral part which also consisted of some ten subects. If we managed to pass that also, we received our diploma. My friend Edith, whom I had known from Kindergarten on, and I studied together as we had for years. We stayed up late and woke up early, just to get enough studying in. And, we both managed to pass our final exam the first time. Generally, at that time, only about 50–75% of students passed the first time. Not passing the final exam meant that the whole last year had to be repeated. So we were very proud of ourselves. In a way, passing my final exam ended my school years and therefore my childhood, even though my childhood had ended when the war had started. Maybe I should say that my childhood ended again.

Ends of a Childhood

Somehow, it seems that my childhood came to an end at different times. It came to an end when we were deported to Westerbork in a cattle train. It came to an end again when we were deported the second time to Theresienstadt. When we came back to Amsterdam, I became a "child" again in that I was no longer as independent as I had been in the camps. I had the responsibility, there, of keeping our space clean, of going to pick up our food, of mending our clothes and socks or stockings and, in general, "taking care of the household." Apparently what was allowed and even obligatory in the camps was no longer allowed after our return to Amsterdam. In both Westerbork and Theresienstadt I had had certain chores to do because my parents were at work and therefore could not do them. I also just announced where I was going, for example to fetch our food, whereas after our return I had to ask for permission to go somewhere. My parents were very protective and I had to obey. Of course, my childhood did not actually return, not even when I started playing in the street with my playmates, who were anywhere from six to ten years old. They and I became good friends. It came to yet another end when I passed my final exams in the lyceum, because my school years were over or so I thought. But it also ended on another day. I must have been in

the third year of the Amsterdams Lyceum, which would mean
that I was about sixteen. I no longer remember the day of the
week or even the date, but I remember the happening. I had
gone to the living room to find something to read in my parents' bookcases. Sitting on the floor, I took out one book after
another, leafed through some, put them back, read bits and
pieces of others, but could not find anything which interested
me majorly. Then, in taking out a fat book, I saw something
hidden behind it. So, naturally, I pulled it out, carefully, and it
was another book. I thought that it was very strange to find a
book standing behind all the others and couldn't imagine why it
would be in that spot. After all, I was allowed to read anything!
So why would they hide books from me? This was very strange.
The fact alone that it was hidden made me curious. I pulled it
out with its back towards me. When I turned it over to look at
the title, I got an enormous shock. I no longer remember the
title, but there was a picture on the cover of a person who
looked like Death himself. He (or maybe she) was nothing but
skin and bones and the head looked like a skull. I opened the
book and then realized immediately why it had been hidden. It
was a picture book about Auschwitz with many, many photographs and some text. Again, I don't remember the text; I suppose it told about Auschwitz. In any event I read it through and
looked at all the photographs, sitting on that floor and prepared
any minute, if my mother or father were to come in, to put the
book back behind the others. Now I knew why it had been hidden. And why my parents had never told me anything about
this concentration camp. I also realized that if Auschwitz
looked like that, there could be, and probably were, other
camps which looked like that with inmates who looked like
Death. It was no longer a secret why so many people had not
come back. All of a sudden I understood what was meant by
"the East" or "Poland" about which we had spoken in the
camps. I understood what had happened to my friend Hans
when he and his family had been transported out of Theresienstadt to "Poland." I understood intellectually that I would

never see him again; that he was gone for good. I understood intellectually that he had been murdered. Anyone who lets people get to such a skeleton state obviously murdered them, perhaps not by shooting them, but certainly by starvation. My head understood all of that. Unfortunately, my emotions didn't. It was too much of a shock, too much of a blinding insight, all at once. I locked it away with all the other emotions and things I could not talk about and, once again, threw out the key.

When I had finished the book—it was quite a thin book—I put it back exactly where and how I had found it. I never told my parents that I had found it, never told them the conclusions I had drawn, the understanding I had gained, never said a word about it at all, exactly as they had not said anything about it when they acquired the book. Just as they had not wanted me to see it and worry about what it showed, so I did not want them to know that I had, in fact, found and seen the book so that they wouldn't worry about my reaction to it.

If my memory serves me well, the book had not shown or said anything about gas chambers. I thought that the Germans simply starved people to death; it did not then occur to me that they also murdered people directly. And, of course, the silence endured. Nobody explained anything, nobody talked about anything and I was left to figure things out alone. In this case, the figuring out was not difficult. I already knew that the Germans had wanted all of us Jews dead. We had been in two concentration camps; obviously there were many more and some looked like Auschwitz, maybe even many. That meant that their inmates looked like the pictures of the Auschwitz inmates as well. Just one more confirmation of the flaw of being Jewish. What tiny bit might have remained of my childhood was now irremediably gone. In fact, my childhood had just died there, in that spot, sitting on the floor in front of that bookcase.

On several occasions, later, I took out the book again, always when I was alone in the apartment. I made sure that my parents never found out that I had found the book, had read it and had looked at it again and again. The pictures never changed, of course, but my rage grew every time I looked at them. It was a rage which I could not show, but that doesn't mean that it didn't exist. It had not begun with the Auschwitz book; it had begun early in the war and had grown on the cattle train to Westerbork. It grew some more in Theresienstadt and now, with this discovery, it was as though it wanted to eat me alive. But I could not talk about it, because talking about the war and the camps was forbidden. So it stayed inside of me for many years, until I found a therapist in 1985 and could, finally, talk about it.

The book about Auschwitz not only made me grow up in a hurry—grow up more—but it also made me angrier than I was anyway. I think that was the first time I was able to identify anger as an emotion. As mentioned before, I was still numb and would remain so for many years, but my anger came through loud and clear. It was born, as a distinct feeling, in that moment when I saw that book. As a teenager, I was often angry and mostly didn't know why or about what. The just mentioned insight did not come until many, many years later. Part of that early anger was also the feeling of not being safe. That brings up the question: "What is 'safe'?"

What if I don't do my homework; what will happen? What if I choose the wrong birthday present for someone? What if I wear the wrong color? What if I quarrel with someone? If I come home and nobody is there, am I still safe? What about people in uniform? If I can't identify the uniform, how will I know that that person is O.K.?

"Safe" is coming home to my parents and finding them both at home. "Safe" is knowing the language of the country where I live. "Safe" is not speaking German in the street. "Safe" is hearing Dutch around me. "Safe" is knowing that the bell will not ring in the middle of the night. "Safe" is knowing that there are no more soldiers who wish me ill. "Safe" is knowing that there will be no air alarm in the night. That I won't be awakened in the middle of the night to go to a hiding place, that I AM in a safe place. "Safe" is having friends who don't think I'm weird or crazy because, when there is a sudden noise, I jump three feet. "Safe" is not attracting attention.

Has all that changed over the years? Well…no. Even today (and as I write this, it is now 2002), if there is a sudden noise, I jump. Even today, if someone rings the doorbell loudly or knocks on the door, I need to see who is there before I open. Even today, when I see a soldier in uniform, or anyone else in uniform, I want to run and hide. Even today, I wonder about people: *Would they hide me? Would they feed me?* So what does "safe" mean today?

"Safe" is coming home and closing the electronic gate behind me, then locking the door. "Safe" is when it gets dark, because in darkness I cannot be seen and therefore nothing can happen to me. Unfortunately, darkness is also unsafe, even dangerous, because I cannot see who is out there. "Safe" is when it grows light, because I can see what's happening and who is maybe at the door. Unfortunately light is also unsafe, even dangerous, because I can be seen; someone may come after me.

In a poem, written some years ago, I consider Darkness my brother, Light my sister. They are always with me, both threatening and both providing safety. They are part of my being. Finally, even today, when I get lost because I've missed a turn-off, or I've misread a map, I get angry. The anger comes out instead of the fear. I loathe getting lost; after all, I might never again be found. I may never find myself again. Even today, when I hear the police sirens or the firefighters' sirens or an ambulance, I want to run and hide. Even today, when someone comes up behind me without making noise, and touches me, I jump three feet (or more). Even today, anger is my first and strongest emotion. In 1985, I wrote a short essay about anger; I am adding it here.

Anger

Anger is a searing orange flame which consumes me. Anger is a hot ocean washing over me and leaving me ice cold and trembling. Anger makes me feel ugly because it is an ugly, gnarled dwarf, attacking me.

It's been inside of me for years, mostly suppressed but occasionally blown out like lava out of a volcano. I never knew why it was there, only that it was part of me, a part I did not like. I tried to get over it by suppressing it more and it wouldn't work. Now I think I know why it's there, although I don't yet know how to handle it.

I'm angry because I lost my grandparents before I ever really knew them. I'm angry because I lost the parents who might have been, had the war not intervened and changed them to what they became. I'm angry because a huge part of my childhood was taken away from me and the child I could have been is now just a phantom. I'm angry because my past was taken away from me; because the adults in my childlife kept telling me that I couldn't understand; that I can't remember and that I didn't notice. But it's not just *their* memories which are correct. *Mine* are correct, too; they're just different because I saw the same things from a child's perspective. Things which didn't frighten them did frighten me; things which happened to me did not happen to them. I'm angry because by discounting my memories and my experiences, they made them seem of no account and therefore made *me* seem of no account.

I'm angry because they tried to "spare" me by not talking about the war and the camps. And I'm in pain for all these same reasons. The anger and the pain are one. I'm angry and I'm hurt because they said and say that Westerbork and Theresienstadt were not so bad; the first was "just" a holding camp and the second was for the elite. But in a holding camp you're not just held; you're held until you're sent on. And I don't know why any of us was "elite." It's not elite to be starved. It's not elite to be behind barbed wire, unfree, except to go to work in a mica

Above:
My mother, age
fifty-eight, and
father, age sixty-
four, in 1988.

Left:
My mother and
father, 1960s.

factory which kills as surely as typhus does. It's not elite to have fleas and bedbugs and no clothes in freezing weather. All of that happened to all of us but no one wanted to talk about it later.

I'm angry and I'm hurt because I lost my friends even if they did not die. I'm angry because there were too many losses and too many deprivations which too few people recognize because I was "only" a child.

The anger and the pain are a time bomb inside of me. Sometimes the bomb explodes but it's for the wrong reasons, reasons which have nothing to do with the war. And after the explosion, the timebomb is still there, still in my belly like a fire that eats away my innards and should be quenched. I think that only tears can quench the fire but there are none yet, although I seem to hover on the brink always. The brink of tears is also the brink of an abyss and I am afraid of it. If I fall in, will I be able to climb back out?

The tears come closer all the time, though, and maybe some time soon they'll wash away that choking feeling that I have, so that the anger and the pain can be washed away as well.

That was in 1985. As of now (2002), it hasn't happened. Nothing much has changed. There have been no tears and even if there had been, they wouldn't have washed away anything. The time bombs of both anger and pain are still inside of me but now I know that they will never go away. They still explode for the wrong reasons; today we have a name for it: "inappropriate anger." Does the name matter? No, not really because it's still the same emotion. The anger masks everything else; it takes the place of fear, grief, non-understanding, pain and many other things. Only I have learned to handle it all a little, a very little, better. But one thing has changed: I now know where it comes from and am, therefore, more able to brush it aside, to not pay too much attention to it, to let it "flow through." As I found out, after 1985, many, if not all, Child Survivors live with that same rage and that same pain. It will never go away but we have learned to live with it. Somewhat, anyway.

ᴄ Emotions

For the longest time, the only emotion I could either show or feel within me was that anger I've just talked about. It was a burning inside of me, an unidentified feeling which I held back most of the time, because I was afraid that, once unleashed, it would either burn me up completely or it would never be quenched at all. It was a rage which would not go away, but when I was a teenager I didn't know either that it was rage or where it came from or what to do with it. It was just *there*. Thus it just stayed within me and blocked whatever other emotions I might have wanted to feel if I had known that there was such a thing as emotions. I had no clue that one was supposed to or could feel more than I did or how to go about feeling emotions. I had no clue that others were able to feel emotions other than anger. My emotions had been suppressed for practically my whole life, throughout emigration, immigration, war, and concentration camps so it was no wonder that they simply stayed away. Part of that was the war, part of it was the imprisonment in the two concentration camps and their humiliations, part of it was the way children were then brought up. I was not allowed to laugh loudly in public, not allowed to cry in public or to shout or to make other noise. I had to be seen but not heard, not only in my childhood but throughout my teen years and after.

Many years later, after I had "discovered" the Child Survivors, I also discovered that many, if not most, children of originally German parents had had the same upbringing as I and thus were not allowed as children to make noise, laugh aloud, cry aloud—in short, they also had to be seen but not heard. At that time I also learned that many, if not most, of the Child Survivors had been unable to talk about their experiences, either because nobody wanted to listen or because they had been told not to talk about them. Children such as I had been, and also children who had been in hiding, were often unable to cry, since in many cases they had been taught not to cry, not to make a sound, because it could cost them their lives. Children as young as two years old had been taught to sit still all day, not to make any noise, not to cry. And they did just what they were taught. Unfortunately for all of us, those early lessons have remained.

I had, perhaps as a result of having been in the camps or perhaps as a result of the war, great difficulty feeling closeness to others. (This is also true of other Child Survivors, for the same reasons, no doubt.) My early lessons had taught me—and taught me very well—that if you get close to someone, you lose that person. I had been close to Max and he had disappeared from one day to the next. I had been close to Hans and he was transported to the East. I had been close to my friend Peggy and she had, like Max, disappeared from one day to the next. I had been close to my grandparents and they were lost to me because they committed suicide, because of Nazism. I had been close to my parents and, though I didn't lose them physically, I lost the parents they might have been. The war and the camps changed them so that they were unrecognizable thereafter. I felt close to my friend Edith, but that went together with the fear that I would lose her also. Together with this fear of inevitable loss went a difficulty in saying goodbye.

When Tante Ulle leaves to go home, will I ever see her again? When Papi goes to that pharmacy meeting he's been talking about, will he come back? If he doesn't, will we know what happened to him? When

I go home from Edith's house, is she still going to be there tomorrow? When Mami goes to do her marketing, will she come home? What if she doesn't? When I go to the store, are Papi and Mami still going to be there when I return? Are they still going to be there when I come home from school? Or are they going to disappear like Omi (my grandmother Marta who lived with us and who had committed suicide in Westerbork)*?*

When my Tante Ulle came for a visit the first time, about two years after the war, she cried when she left. Thus I found out that I was not the only one to have trouble saying good-bye. The difference between us was that I didn't cry—I didn't know how. Tante Ulle cried at every goodbye for the rest of her life, trying to hide that fact by putting on sunglasses even when it was pouring with rain. I still have trouble saying goodbye, even today. I am still not sure that I will see the other person again when we separate, even today. The very worst goodbye, though, is the one that isn't, the one you don't get to say because someone has suddenly died or has left permanently, without saying anything, to some other place. That kind of non-goodbye leaves me crippled emotionally, and, again, this is true for many other Child Survivors. It is, in fact, a sort of un-safeness, an un-safeness which comes out in all sorts of what I now call "idiosyncrasies" for lack of a better term.

Even today, I still jump at sudden noises. Even today, I cringe when I see people in uniform, even if they are not soldiers. Even today, if the bell rings suddenly, day or night, it gives me the shivers. Even today, when I hear the police or the firefighters' sirens, I want to race to a shelter. Even today, when people come up behind me so quietly that I do not hear them, and that person touches me when I do not expect it, I jump. And even today, I do not think that "safe" is easy to come by.

There was, in my childhood, so much fear that it never went completely away, even many years later. Throughout my teen years, there was fear of doing things wrong or dropping and breaking things. There was the fear that I might not exist. There was the fear that, even if I did exist, I had the wrong

shape, the wrong height, the wrong voice, the wrong everything. As I grew up more, some of that fear receded. But not all
of it. To this day, I never know whether I say the right thing or
know what to say. What do you say, after you've said "Hello"?
How do you make conversation?

Then there are also the "idiosyncrasies" which come out,
often, at the most inconvenient times and places. For example:
A friend and I were walking and, on our walk, saw a clearly
defined, rectangular open space with overturned earth in front
of a newly erected building. My friend said: "*I wonder what
they'll put up here?*" My reaction? "*I hope it's not a mass grave.*"
Why should it be? Why would it be? But it was my first, instinc-
tive reaction. Other than saying things, there are also the things
I see. In New York, on a public transport bus, I saw a sign in a
shop that said, I thought, "*Chains.*" "*Why would anyone sell
chains? Do they put them on others? Do they make them walk with
chains?*" In actual fact, the sign in the window of a jewelry store
said: "Sale of neck chains." On that same bus, I saw a man come
in, a new passenger, who had a black briefcase in one hand and
something longish under the other arm. I took one look at him
and was immediately scared to death: "*Oh, my God, he's got a
gun!*" I slid down in my seat, trying to hide, but unable to. I was
sure that he was going to shoot me. He didn't. What was the
gun? It was a rolled-up umbrella!

Reactions like that don't make for ease of living. They keep
you constantly on your toes, in a state of almost constant aware-
ness of what goes on around you. This does not make for peace
of mind. Then there is the counterpart of the earlier rage and
fear sometimes to today's reactions. It is extremely difficult to
be carefree, to enjoy time with friends without other thoughts.
As a teenager I cannot remember ever having felt real joy. Of
course, there were joyful occasions such as birthdays or going
on to the next grade in school or people coming to visit. But a
joy which lasts? I don't remember any at that time. There was
also no real happiness. I was too afraid that it would be taken
away in some way, so I didn't dare have any. Yes, of course I was

happy with a good grade, but I was also afraid that I would ruin it by making too many mistakes the next time. I was much, much more at home with feeling fear and rage. Those I knew. I knew what they would do to me. I had no idea what joy and happiness would do to me. And I didn't dare try. As a result, my fellow students found me "too serious" or "too dull." That lasted through my time at university and after. It didn't change until 1985 when I found the earlier-mentioned therapist and worked on realizing that joy is O.K. and so is happiness, even for someone like me, a Holocaust Child Survivor.

Unfortunately, anger is still my overriding emotion. But at least the others exist now and I accept them. That is progress.

⌒ *CARE Packages and Other Things*

From the time I was in Elementary School, all the way through High School, we received CARE packages. As mentioned before, nothing much was available in Holland, and people from the USA began sending us CARE packages. CARE was—and is—an organization which was founded in 1945 when twenty-two American organizations formed a cooperative to rush life-saving CARE packages to survivors of World War II. The cooperative has always been known by its acronym *CARE*. Originally, in 1945, that stood for *Cooperative for American Remittances to Europe*. Today, however, the same acronym stands for *Cooperative for Assistance and Relief Everywhere, Inc.* It was then an organization through which people could send packages with badly needed supplies to families in Europe who, after the war, had nothing. Eventually American families could "adopt" a family somewhere in Europe to whom they then could send regular packages. So we were "adopted" by an American family who sent us not only luxuries like coffee and sugar but also and mainly clothes, soap, toothpaste and such things. The American family must have had three daughters because all the clothes I received from their packages came in three's, all in different sizes. I got three differently sized skirts, three blouses, three sweaters, and so on. My mother also received clothes, but for my father there were none, either because the American father did not wear the same size as my father or perhaps because there was no longer a father; this I don't know. I do know that, very early in these sendings, there was a skirt, blue and white plaid, which grew with me. I wore it in Elementary School at age twelve and still wore it at Het Amsterdams Lyceum at age sixteen. There were also some sweaters which grew along with me. One was deep pink and one was dark green. They were, of course, the same model and brand, just different sizes and colors. The third sweater I don't remember, perhaps we gave it to someone else. But the pink and the green I started wearing at about thirteen years of age and I still had and wore them at twenty-one. For me, these were, of course, new clothes and, after the war when we had literally nothing besides the camp clothes we wore, they were very welcome indeed. Besides, they were very different from the clothes then being worn in Holland. They were much more colorful than the Dutch clothes and the patterns were different. To me they were new and exotic and exciting and I loved them. One of the blouses had a name on a corner of the collar, Sue. I had no idea then that it was a first name, how to pronounce it or what it meant, but it was different and it came from far away, therefore it was exotic and it was new to me.

Mami?

Yes!

What does this word mean? And how do you pronounce it? Why is it on the collar?

I don't know. I've never seen it before, so I don't know either how to pronounce it. It could be a name.

But why would there be a name on the collar? If that girl is my age, surely she knows what her name is.

I never did figure out why the name was on the blouse or how to pronounce it. Eventually, about five years later, when more things had become available, I actually received really new clothes, clothes which were bought specially for me. I remember two dresses: the first was bought in a shop owned by friends of my parents' whom I called "oom," uncle and "tante," aunt, as was the custom then in Europe. The dress, which I was allowed to choose, had a background of yellow and had horizontal and vertical stripes of other colors. It was wool and had short sleeves. I named it the "Tante Suse dress" because it was bought from Tante Suse and because it was a way to make it distinguished. I must not have grown and filled out much at that time, because I still had it when I was twenty-one. I had received it when I was about seventeen. It was the very first brand-new dress I had and that was exciting and wonderful. The other one was, in my eyes, very fashionable: it had a dark brown pleated skirt and the top part was beige with dark brown flowers sewed on diagonally across the chest. I must have kept that dress also for a very long time because I remember wearing my first pair of high heels with it.

In spite of this evidence of growing up, I really wasn't as grown up as it seems. My parents did not, as mentioned, talk about the war or discuss those times. They told me to think of the future and encouraged me to work hard in school. Yet when I was fifteen and began to play with the neighborhood children in the street, they did not keep me from it. Children in Amsterdam always played in the street when they didn't have a garden and most apartments did not. I had played in the street before the war and now went back to it. My playmates at this time were anywhere between six and ten years old. They knew that I was older. I knew that I was older. But none of us cared. After the first few times, the children came to our door, rang the bell and then asked what we always asked:

Mag Gaby buiten spelen? May Gaby come out and play?

We played what children, from time immemorial, have played: hide-and-seek, catch, rope skipping, tops, ball games and so on. In actual fact fifteen-year-olds didn't play in the street anymore nor did they play such games; those were children's games but I enjoyed them and I enjoyed the children's companionship. I wasn't the leader, I was just one of them. Was I trying to re-find my childhood? Probably, but I didn't know that then; it just felt right. As it had started, so it stopped after maybe six months. Nothing was ever said about it by my parents at any time. Perhaps if I had not had friends of my own age, they might have said something, but I did have friends of my own age, my classmates and some children of my parents' friends. Perhaps, also, my parents did not see any harm in my playing outside, as long as I also did my schoolwork.

☞ *Trip to Lugano*

One summer, during my lyceum years, my parents arranged for me to go to Lugano, in Italian Switzerland, for my summer vacation from school. Why Lugano? Because my Tante Ulle, Aunt Ulle, my mother's sister, lived there and could keep an eye on me. Tante Ulle had been sent to Lugano in 1939, by the company she worked for in Berlin. All employees had to spend time in the Lugano office and in 1939 it was my Tante Ulle's turn. When it was her time to return to Berlin, she did not go back because the situation there, under Hitler, was so very bad. She stayed in Lugano, illegally, found some sort of job and ended up staying in Lugano for the rest of her life, eventually getting Swiss citizenship. This visit to her was to be, at the same time, a sort of exchange visit. I was to stay with an Italian-speaking family and then, the next summer, the son of the family where I had stayed would come to stay with us in Amsterdam. As previously with the trip to Denmark, I was not consulted about this, I was not asked whether I wanted to go, I was simply told. Again, I did not want to go. This was another separation and, like all separations, it frightened me. After all, I reasoned, suppose something happens to my parents, and I have to stay in Lugano forever? Again, I would have to learn a different language and different customs. This time, though,

the trip was made by airplane. Friends of my parents' had a
son, a few years younger than I, and Peter and I travelled together. The first thing that happened was that Peter lost his
plane ticket. I had been told that I was responsible for him (I
was all of fourteen) and so, of course, I thought it was my fault
that he lost it. It didn't occur to me that he didn't remember
where he had put it; since I was responsible for him, it was obviously my fault. Eventually, however, Peter found that he had
just mislaid his ticket, not lost it totally. I breathed a sigh of relief. In Zurich we were to be met by both the family with
whom Peter would be staying and by my Tante Ulle. Well,
when we got to the airport in Zurich, his family was indeed
there—but my aunt was not. I looked around everywhere; I
knew her since she had visited us in Amsterdam the previous
year, so I knew what she looked like. Nobody was to be found.
People kept leaving the airport and eventually Peter and his
family had to leave as well. There I was, alone in a strange
country with no idea how to get to Lugano. Eventually my
aunt showed up and said that she had missed her train. We
climbed into the train to Lugano and the journey continued.
From Zurich to Lugano, then, took four hours by train. We
talked off and on and at one moment a train passed us on another set of rails. The train had a lot of freight cars at its end.
Tante Ulle began to explain what these were used for and to
her surprise and, I suppose, to her horror, I said:

   *Oh, I know what those are. We travelled in cattle cars when we
went to the camp.*

   After that, my aunt was quiet for a long time. After our arrival in Lugano, I stayed with Tante Ulle for a few days, before
she took me to the family I was to stay with. I don't remember
what we did during those days, except for one day when she
took me to what we would now call a supermarket. I had never
seen such a thing! It was so big and so bright and so clean. And
all that food! Holland was still dirt poor and the shops did not
have anything much to sell. We had ration coupons, but no
merchandise. Here, in Lugano, not only were there no ration

coupons, but the market was full to bursting with all sorts of food, most of which I didn't know, had never seen before.

What a big shop! And so much food ! You could feed a whole camp with all of that and nobody would go hungry! Why is there so much? Who needs all that food? How do you buy it? There are so many different things. Do you have to choose? Then, how do you do that? How do you know what you want? What is the difference between two kinds of meat? How do you know what vegetable to choose? It's really easier, in a way, at home, because you just take what's there.

My aunt offered to buy me a bar of chocolate but I didn't even answer her. I was mute with fear that I had to choose something and I didn't know what to do. She ended up just choosing one big bar. What frightened me in the market was actually the freedom. The freedom to choose, to leave what you didn't want, to buy what you did want. And the fact that there was such a multitude of things. I had never seen any shop like that, overflowing with merchandise. Obviously this was a land of plenty—but I couldn't understand that as yet. I had very much still a camp mindset, even though it was now two years later.

The next day Tante Ulle took me to the family who would be my host for the next few weeks. In the process of delivering me there, she took out the bar of chocolate and told the mother and the daughter of that family that I would be happy to share this with them. I dared not say anything, but in actual fact I wasn't at all happy to share the chocolate. It was *mine*, she had bought it for *me* and I did *not* want to share. But I dared not say so because it would be gainsaying an adult. And I had been taught that that wasn't right. So I said nothing and I did share, but I resented it fiercely. Until then I had not ever had anything which I could or should share so this was also a new kind of act for me.

In the year 2000, I wrote a poem about ration coupons and what we could and could not do with them. I add it here:

AFTER THE WAR

Before the war
I was too little:
a small child of six years old.
I don't remember times before the war
when everything was plentiful.
I only remember times of war
and times after the war
when nothing was plentiful.

After the war,
when times were "normal" again,
my Mami and my Papi and I,
we had rationing coupons for meat,
but there was no meat;
coupons for eggs and milk,
but eggs and milk were nonexistent;
coupons for "textiles,"
but there were no dresses for Mami,
no suits for Papi, no coat for me
in the empty stores.

We had coupons for sugar,
but sugar could not be found,
nor chocolate or sweets for us children.
We had coupons for everything
though money for nothing
and nothing was available
in the empty stores.

After the war,
I had out-grown clothes,
Mami and Papi had worn-out clothes,
but nothing to repair them with.
Then we received CARE packages
and I got everything in three's:
three skirts, three blouses, three sweaters,
all identical except in size.
I wore the smallest at age twelve,
the largest when I was twenty-one
and I was happy to have them.
I had a party dress of red plaid,
made from rustling taffeta.
IT came from a little girl like me
who, unlike me, had died in the war.
Her dress went to Terezín's "Kleiderkammer"*
from where I received it,
paid for in years of imprisonment.
I wore it for many years
because I loved it so.

We had no coupons for toys
and no toys for me
until my aunt came to visit two years later
and brought me a net with
three red and yellow bouncing balls:
a toy for a six-year-old.
I was delighted!
I was fourteen!

* *Kleiderkammer*: clothing warehouse

We had no coupons for family
and had no family left:
I had no grandparents,
no great uncles or aunts, no cousins at all.
They were all murdered
and even if coupons had existed for family
and even if we had had them,
there would have been no family;
they were dead and lost forever.

We had no coupons for kindness,
yet kindness was plentiful:
our neighbors, a family of four,
took us in with open arms,
found space in their apartment,
space at their table,
stretched their scanty resources
to feed three more mouths
and always managed
and never complained.
They are the true heroes.

We had no coupons for education,
for learning, reading, studying,
yet studying was plentiful,
in grade five (at age twelve),
in extra lessons by a tutor,
in trying to make up lost time
but never succeeding.
Time lost remains lost.

Today,
we have no coupons for memories,
but our memories are plentiful;
no coupons for pain
or for present reactions to past events,
yet pain and reactions are plentiful;
no coupons nor rationing for rage,
yet our rage is plentiful and fierce,
burningly hot, bitingly acidic,
always with us,
the one companion we do not want.

I had some trouble in Lugano, because only the lady of the household spoke some German and I did not speak any Italian. The son, who was later to come to Amsterdam to stay with us, spoke some German but very little. The father and sister spoke no German at all. Both the son and the daughter were older than I, the daughter by about a year and the son by maybe two or three years. He was, therefore, seventeen to my fourteen and had no interest whatsoever in making friends with me. As I had not been asked about this, so he had not been asked either, nor had his sister. I doubt that they particularly wanted a stranger in their house who, moreover, could not talk to them. The girl was about fifteen and much more developed, both physically and mentally, than I was. I must have looked like a real child to her. She, also, made no attempts to be friendly. And neither did I because I did not know how.

I stayed with the family for about six weeks and then returned home, again by plane, but this time with no responsibility for anyone else. I no longer remember how Peter came home. I just knew that I was happy to be home, where I could make myself understood and where I could understand everyone. I could once again try to regrow the earlier roots I had had in Amsterdam. I was home, where I belonged!

↝ *Edith*

Eventually my six weeks were up and I was able to go home to Amsterdam. It was, again, a big change: from plenty to almost nothing. The year was 1947 or 1948 and Holland had not yet recovered from the war. It would take many long years more for the country and the people to really recover—if we ever did. At that time, we still had rationing coupons (which lasted till at least 1950) and nothing much could be bought. To come back from Switzerland, where food was pressed upon me all the time, to Holland, where there was practically none, was an extreme change.

Perhaps here is the occasion to talk about my friend Edith. As mentioned before, we had known each other since kindergarten; we went to the same Montessori kindergarten which was close to both our apartments. But as small children we were not that friendly. I do not, for example, remember going to Edith's house to play. I do not remember her coming to my house or our playing in the street together. My best friend at that time was Carla, my upstairs neighbor. After the war, Carla was two years ahead of me in school (she had not had to miss any time) and, in many ways, more mature than I. She had made friends in her school, and I began making friends as well, albeit very slowly. I knew Edith in Elementary School, but

again not really as a friend. Our school had three sections of
sixth grade because so many children came after the war. As it
so happened, Edith was in one sixth grade class and I was in another. Yet I knew her because she had had polio during the war
and as a result, had a big metal brace on one leg. She could walk
but not too well and came to school on a small children's bicycle, a bright red one. When we both finished Elementary
School, we found ourselves in the same class at the Amsterdams
Lyceum. They had several sections for their beginning class
(what would be seventh grade in the USA). By then she had a
proper adult bike and I had one as well and so we went to school
together. We also became fast friends and began spending time
together and studying together. In order to be fair, we spent
one evening studying at her house, then the next evening at my
house. In winter, my room, which was in the northeast corner
of the apartment house, was bitterly cold. It had a very small
central heater, but in those first post-war years, there was no
coal, thus no heat. So I went to bed, under the warm covers, and
Edith wore as many layers of clothes as she had. The next
evening the situation would be reversed and I would be wearing
as many layers as I had and Edith would be snug in bed.

Edith is a Jewish Child Survivor, as I am. She spent the war
years in hiding in a convent where the nuns took care of her
during her illness with polio. Yet, here we were both Child Survivors and one would think we could talk about what happened
to us. We didn't. I suppose both of us had been taught not to ask
questions, not to ask what happened, and so we never talked
about it at all. I knew that she had been in hiding. She knew that
I had been in the camps. But that was all. Never did we ask for
details or talk about it in any way. We talked about our studies,
we compared notes taken in class, we quizzed each other, we
recited what we had to learn by heart. There was a certain
amount of "girl talk"; we talked about the boys in our class and
about other boys (of whom we did not know many). We talked
about swimming, which we both loved, and about dancing
class, which I loathed. I no longer remember what she thought

Left:
Edith, 1955.

Below:
Edith, her
husband Jan,
and Gabriele.

about that. But about the war, her hiding experience, my camp experience, nothing was said at all. Not long ago, I read in one Dutch survivor newsletter the following: "If you have to be silent, do you then really exist?" And to my mind, you don't. If you have to be silent, if you have to leave things unsaid, untalked about, you do not actually exist. Only a shell exists, but the bigger part of you is elsewhere. The bigger part of you, the most important part is a shadow. In 1985, I wrote a story about just that, about a shadow person. Though it is about myself, I wrote it in the third person because I had not yet learned to face my past straight on.

Shadow

Once upon a time, there was a shadow. This was no ordinary shadow, like any other; no, this was a *Shadow*. The shadow's name was just "Shadow" with nothing before or after. Shadow knew that she had been a girl at one time, but it was too long ago and she couldn't remember what it felt like. Now, she was incorporeal, floating. She had had a substance once, but she had lost it somehow, she couldn't remember how. From that time on she felt that she was transparent. Shadow was the only one to know that; the world in which she lived did not see her as a transparent shadow. Sometimes she tried to remember how it felt to have a substance, but she never could; it was too difficult. The people around her, she saw, had a substance which was important and solid and a shadow which appeared and disappeared. But Shadow was always a shadow; it was all she was, her whole being.

She decided that she would try and find a substance. She was still quite small, but if she obeyed her parents, maybe she would find her lost substance. So she tried to be very good, said "please" and "thank you" when required, went to bed when she was told and always finished all the food on her plate. She set the table and dried the dishes without breaking a single one. She dressed as she was told and studied hard in school. She learned to write and to read. She read lots of books and discovered fairies and witches and magicians. She wrote essays and tried to learn arithmetic, but nothing helped; she remained just Shadow.

Then she started looking for a fairy godmother to help her. She searched in the streets around her house, on a meadow she knew and in the forest near the city. But never did she find one. She continued being a good girl; she went to the dancing lessons to which she was sent but which she did not like, and to the swimming lessons which she did like. She learned how to ride a bicycle. She received a swimming diploma and one for knowing how to ride her bicycle in traffic. She also received a diploma for finishing Elementary School. She wrapped them around herself, thinking that they would make her a substance. But when she looked at herself, she was still only Shadow.

She went to more schools and learned many more things. She made some friends with whom she went bicycling or to the beach or to the movies. She even gave a class party once in her house. But nothing ever changed her and she remained only Shadow. She added more diplomas to the ones she had wrapped around her but she now knew that none of them would fulfill her desire. The substance she sought remained elusive.

Shadow learned a profession at which she was very good. She worked hard and enjoyed what she did. She travelled to other countries and wherever she went she always looked for a fairy godmother to help her, then widened her search to include a magician. Sometimes she thought she had found one but when she told the magician what she needed, it always turned out to be a false magician who could not help her. So she remained just Shadow.

The friends she had made liked her and did not seem to notice anything amiss. But Shadow herself knew what was missing and that without a core she could never be a real person. She could laugh and talk with others; like what they liked or dislike what they disliked. Finally, since nothing she had tried had worked, she decided to do without a substance and give up the search. She unwrapped the diplomas and tidied them away in a drawer. Then she lived as everybody else did. She had friends over for dinner or went out with them. She planted flowers and pulled weeds. She read the newspaper, went shopping and for all the world was indistinguishable from anyone else. But she was still only Shadow.

One day she met a special person and after a while they married. She continued working in her profession; they now saw more friends, they went shopping together, planted flowers together and pulled weeds together. They lived together like everyone else and after some time Shadow became aware that she was no longer quite so transparent. She had gained a little substance but she still felt that she had no core. Her marriage went on for many years but nothing further changed and still she remained only Shadow.

One day she was invited to a special occasion. There, to her great surprise, she met a real magician. She didn't realize it immediately because she had quite given up looking for fairy godmothers or magicians. Real magicians look like other people and it takes time to find them out. It's not easy to do for magicians work quietly and often in secret. They have their own way of doing things. Shadow, some time later, knew that this magician was real because this one could see the transparency. So Shadow gathered all her courage and asked the magician for help in finding her substance. "Yes, I can help you," said the magician, "but you must work as well. I can show you the road, but you must walk it." So it came about that Shadow took a small step forward on this road. And then another small step. The magician did not show her the whole road at once; Shadow would have had too much difficulty following it. But every time the magician indicated a new piece of it, Shadow tried to walk it. She didn't always succeed; sometimes she couldn't see the road; sometimes she saw only grey fog. She stumbled at times or lost her way. At other times she advanced farther than she had believed she could. She found that the road was long and had many obstacles but she did persevere.

Some day there will be no more grey fog and no more obstacles and Shadow will reach the end of her road. On that day she will have found her lost substance and she will no longer be Shadow.

Today, the sessions with the "magician" have long been over, but I have not yet reached the end of my road. The ending of the story is perhaps too optimistic: there is often a grey fog and the road can be and often is very painful. There will always be obstacles, obstacles which may consist of a sight, a smell, a sound which brings back the past instantly. But somewhere along that road, I have learned that these things can happen but that they do not have to determine my life. I know where these "obstacles" come from and I can now send them back to the past where they belong. There will always be days when I am "Shadow" and days when I have a substance. And, most of the time, these days, I do have a substance.

As for my friend Edith, she still lives in Holland. In the beginning of my life here in the United States, we did not correspond too often; both our lives were busy. Now, however, thanks to computers with e-mail, our correspondence is regular. A few years ago I went back to Holland one summer and Edith and I met again, no longer as teenagers but as middle-aged women. But that was the only thing which had changed. Everything else had remained and remains the same, only we have substituted e-mail for the phone calls of our teenage years.

☞ *Teenage Years*

During my teenage years, somehow there was always something wrong with me, physically speaking. As mentioned before, in the first few years of the lyceum, I had appendicitis and therefore an appendectomy, and tonsillitis, and therefore a tonsillectomy. Unfortunately, that wasn't all. Just as in my Elementary School years, so also now, I picked up whatever was going around, was frequently ill and had to miss school. Before the war I had had all the then usual children's diseases: German measles, mumps, chicken pox, whooping cough and so on. In Westerbork, I had had the measles. So that was all over with and I was, from then on, immune. I also had fevers with no known cause, but which caused me to have to stay home and in bed. But at age fifteen, I came down with a strep throat which eventually caused rheumatoid arthritis, or so we were told at that time. As a result, my right hand—which was at that time the only part of me involved—trembled and I could not write clearly. Eventually the trembling went away, but the swelling and the pain remained and over the years, the rheumatoid arthritis has spread and affected other parts of me.

By that time, I was pretty resigned to all of it. It was just something that happened; there was nothing I could do about it. I could do my schoolwork at home; once a teacher even allowed me to take a test at home while I was ill again. I caught up as best I could. In addition to these various illnesses, I was also very shy and still thought of myself as ugly.

I was awkward in my movements; I felt that my arms and my legs were too long. They always seemed to stick out at an angle and I was forever knocking things over. I walked with my hands in my pockets so that my arms wouldn't swing out and possibly hurt someone. This allowed me also to hunch over so that I seemed smaller to myself. I felt heavy and clumsy and never knew how to stand or sit. I was uncomfortable with myself.

My glasses and my braces were also part of that feeling. So even when I was up and about, I was very quiet and didn't say very much, especially when my parents had company. In school, I acted the same way. Some of my fellow students were fond of practical jokes, some were rather loud in class, a number of them liked to horse around and show off. I mostly only answered when I was spoken to or called on by a teacher. The lyceum years were also the years when we girls began to be interested in the boys and vice versa. Some of the boys would, in winter, put snow or ice down the neck of their favorite girl or tease them in other ways. I never could understand why, if you liked someone so much, you had to tease them—but then I was probably behind in that sense as well. On the whole, most of my classmates found me, as they said in Dutch: "sloom," i.e. dull or slow. I was behind with other things as well, or so I thought. Most of the girls I knew had begun menstruating at a fairly early age, and thought of themselves as "young women." Their bodies had also begun to develop.

I am still completely flat, as flat as an ironing board. How can that be? I am seventeen, everyone else looks different. There must be something wrong with my body. I wonder why? The girls also talk about "three days" of pain and discomfort when they have their period. I don't have one. Will I ever get one? What if I don't? Does that mean I won't ever grow up?

Gabriele, 1947, age fourteen.

I talked to my mother about it and she kept reassuring me that things would happen in their own good time—but that didn't help me at all. I couldn't understand how all these girls, some of them younger than I by several years, could know all these things. Again, I did not fit in—at least in my mind. Finally, at age seventeen, I did begin to menstruate and felt incredibly grown up. I also found out that my classmates did not know everything. There was no question of three days; the pain and discomfort began several days before my actual period, lasted through it, all seven days of it, and instead of feeling grown-up, I soon began to dread these days.

Oh, no, not again! Not so soon already! I feel awful, my stomach sticks out and I have headaches all the time. It's all very well for Mami to say that "millions of women have this, you'll get through it," or for Papi to tell me that "it can't be that bad, your mother never has any pain," but it is that bad and the millions of other women don't interest me in the least. I'm the one who has the stomachache, I can't feel theirs. Even lying down doesn't help. Now what do I do? I can't concentrate, so I can't read or do homework. My head hurts all the time! This is horrible!

Instead of feeling that I was growing up, becoming a woman, I just wanted to get "all this" over with. I hated it and saw no use in it. I saw no reason why I had to hurt so much to become a woman.

In any event, so what if I become a woman? Why should that make a difference to me? I'm not even sure I have a future, so why should being a woman make a difference? Mami says that I can then have children. But I won't know what to do with them. Besides, what does that mean: "becoming a woman"? Does that mean that I am all grown up? I sure don't feel that way and nobody treats me as a grown-up. Does it mean I have to get married? With whom? One of the boys of my class? They are just children, just like me. I don't know what they mean by "becoming a woman."

There were all sorts of questions going through my mind. I knew that I didn't really know how to play. So how could I play with any future children? I had grown up during war times and in concentration camps. Would, therefore, my children grow up that way? In Theresienstadt, my friend Hans and I had talked about getting married "after the war." But when "after the war" came, Hans was dead, or at least he had disappeared from my horizon.

So how can I fall in love with anybody? What's that like anyway? I love Hans; does that mean I can't love anyone else? How do you fall in love? How does it feel? Can you feel anything? I don't normally feel very much, so how would I know if I am in love? The boys in my class are just friends, I can't see them as anything else. Besides, don't you have to be an adult to be in love? I'm not an adult; I may never get there.

It was just one more thing to worry about, one more thing I couldn't change. If I couldn't or didn't fall in love, then that would be yet another flaw in me, so I thought. At that time, I didn't even think about marriage or romance or anything like that. I suppose I stayed away from it, even in daydreams, because I had no idea what all it involved, how these things began. I saw the teasing in school, but saw no connection between the boys' teasing of a special girl and the liking of a girl. To me they didn't go together. I knew one thing, though, I didn't want "to be taken care of" as one was supposed to be in marriage. I had learned early that I couldn't count on that or on anyone; taking care of me was up to me, not up to someone else, be that a boyfriend or a husband.

As I have mentioned, my experience in the camps has made me wary of getting close to people. I had been close to Hans and he had been sent to Auschwitz and murdered there. I had been close to Max and he had disappeared. I had been close to Omi Marta and she died. I had been close to my parents and, though they did not disappear physically, they were so changed as to be unrecognizable.

Equally I had enormous difficulties with saying goodbye, even just to go to school. Again, my early experiences had taught me—and taught me very well—that if you say goodbye to someone, you probably will never see that person again.

*When I come home from school, will everybody still be there?
After school, if I call Edith, will she still be there? If Papi leaves for
this business trip that he was talking about, will he come back? If he
doesn't, will we ever know what happened to him? When Edith goes
home after we have studied, will she come to school tomorrow? Will
she still be there?*

When my aunt, my mother's sister, came to visit a few years
after the war, I found out that I was not the only one who had
trouble saying goodbye. When she left, she was crying and, in
later years, till the end of her life, she never got over that. She
had as much trouble with saying goodbye as I did at that time
and as I still do. The years have not changed that; saying goodbye is always difficult and will likely be so until I die. The worst
is, though, when someone dies or leaves permanently and you
don't get to say goodbye. That leaves you almost crippled,
emotionally.

I loved to swim and often went to the public pool where I had
learned to swim while I was still in Elementary School. There I
saw the same kind of teasing that I saw at school, and to my surprise, the girls I saw there seemed to like these pranks. I did not
see anything of this kind, however, in the riding school where I
took riding lessons. I had always loved horses and used to ask
my parents for a horse on every birthday that passed.

*Mami, may I have a horse for my birthday? Just a small one? I'll
take care of it, I promise.*

My mother's usual answer was: *And where do you think we
would keep it—in the living room? And who is going to clean up after
it?*

That didn't hinder me from dreaming about having a horse
and riding. My beloved Karl May books helped that dream,
too. If I dreamed of anything in those days, it was of riding a
wild horse, a mustang just like "Old Shatterhand" (one of the
characters in the Karl May books) rode. If I couldn't have a
horse—and even I had to admit that my mother's argument

made sense!—then I dreamed of riding lessons, of actually sitting on top of a horse, giving it instructions and commands and having it do what I wanted.

When I was about fifteen, I don't remember my exact age, I was allowed to take riding lessons. My father and I went off to the riding school, the Vondel *manege*, so called because it was located in the Vondel Straat (Vondel Street) in order to sign me up. I was put in the group of beginners whom everybody called "the little ones," because most of them were quite young. I stuck out in that group because I was not only much older but also much taller than the actual children. For once it didn't matter; I was so happy to finally be able to climb on a horse that I didn't care about being different. Once a week I went, on my bicycle, to the riding school to have my lesson. I felt really powerful on those horses. Just to sit on a horse, without its going anywhere, was joy and contentment. We learned to ride straight on, to trot, to canter, to ride in figure eights, to turn around, to stop properly. The lessons were always over far too fast and then we had to climb down and wait another week for another lesson.

But after the actual riding lessons, there were other lessons: we had to clean the front hooves of the horses, learn to put their saddle and bridle on and take them off and, in summer, give the horses a bath. I loved every minute of it. I could have spent all day, every day, there. Naturally, the lessons didn't go without accidents. We had to ride a different horse every time, so that we could get used to all sorts. Not all the horses were necessarily obedient. So it was that on several occasions I was thrown off but had to climb back up immediately. I didn't mind any of that, I loved all of it. It was also possible, indeed probable, that in cleaning hooves, the horse would step on one of my feet and cause a big bruise. When I came home, my mother, who did not like horses at all and was even afraid of them, would say:

Pfooi, you smell of horse! Go take a bath right away!

I didn't mind the smell but my mother hated it.

Even after I had been diagnosed with rheumatoid arthri-

tis—then just called "rheumatism"—I continued the riding lessons. The exercise was good and I was not shy with the horses. I
got along a lot better with animals than with people at that
time. With animals I didn't need to be afraid; with people I was
afraid all the time. Animals don't disagree with you, they don't
answer back, they don't require that you telephone them and
they don't care if you don't always talk to them. So my rapport
with animals was very good.

Throughout my teen years, there were again a lot of things
I didn't know, that I either did not remember or had never
known. What had happened when I was given chocolate at our
homecoming happened again and again. One occasion I remember very clearly was the following: I was walking with my
mother in the Scheldestraat (the Schelde Street) when we
passed a green grocer. I looked at the different kinds of fruit he
had in his boxes outside and saw something I had never seen before. I stopped my mother and asked:

*Mami, look at that. What is that, that yellow thing? Is that a
fruit? Where does it come from? I've never seen anything like it. It
has a funny shape. Can you eat it?*

My mother smiled and answered:

You really are *a war child. That "yellow thing" is a banana and,
yes, it is a fruit. It comes from overseas; we don't get it here out of season.*

Another lady, walking near us, overheard my question and I
can still see her face which clearly showed what she was thinking: "That poor child, she must be retarded." She didn't over-
hear the answer, however, so she never changed her mind about
all this. It was a typical example of all the things I did not know;
I asked that kind of question for many years to come. It didn't
help, of course, that we could only see or buy bananas and other
fruit like that in season. All citrus fruit and bananas were im-
ported and lasted only as long as the season lasted; after that
they were gone until the next year.

As my teen years passed, my school work took up more and
more time. Edith and I studied together every day, both for the

Left:
Gabriele, 1947,
age fourteen.

Below:
Gabriele, 1950,
age seventeen.

daily work and for the final exam after the last year. Homework took up hours every day. Eventually the final year came around and we studied even more than before. The final exam was—as it always was—extremely difficult, in part because there were so many subjects to know and in part because, after all, this was the end of the lyceum years. After this, people went on to university or whatever they wanted to do. By great good luck and by many, many hours of studying, both Edith and I passed the final exam the first time. After the results had been announced, I said to my parents:

I am never, ever, going to take another exam, for anything.

My parents didn't laugh, but they also didn't answer. And, of course, I ended up taking all sorts of exams, later in my university years.

⌒ *Dancing Lessons and*
Other Problems

While I was still a teenager or, as we then said, adolescent, there were a great number of things which frightened me. In hindsight I suppose that it was life in general which frightened me. I didn't grow very fast, no doubt a result of the so-called nutrition in the camps, but my body did, eventually, slowly, develop. Whether that frightened me or whether it was life in general, I don't know, but I walked, usually, with my head down and my hands in my pockets. I felt that my arms and legs were too long for my body, I was clumsy at best, falling over things and dropping things and bumping into the furniture. So I thought that if I kept my hands in my pockets, at least I couldn't do any harm with my too long arms.

This is a good coat for me, the pockets are nice and deep and I can put my hands in the pockets. That way, I can't knock anything about. Besides, it's a raincoat, so I can wear it all the time. It is a bit big but that means that it covers me completely. I can't swing my arms, the way Papi and Mami say I should. I'll just bump into people or knock things off tables. And then what? What if I break a glass? What if I hurt somebody?

I no longer remember whether that raincoat was my only

coat or whether it just rained a lot at that time (because in Holland it always does rain a lot). But in any event I was happy with the coat.

I looked down to the street mostly because I was afraid of meeting someone I knew.

If I see anyone, I have to make conversation and I never know how to do that. What do I say? I can say hello, of course, but then what? Do I ask after their children? Or say that my parents would be happy to see them? I never know the right thing.

If I didn't see anybody, then that eliminated that particular problem. So I looked at the street and went around not seeing people. This lasted from the time I was about fourteen until the end of my schooldays, at twenty.

Shortly after we had our own apartment back, my father had to go to England for business. When he came back, he brought me back a bicycle.

A bicycle! Wonderful! And such a light one, too! Much lighter than the typical Dutch bicycles. Oh, this is marvellous, I'll get to school so much faster! And everyone else has one too.

It was a Raleigh bike, fairly small and just right in size. It provided a lot of freedom for me, since I could now go for "een stukje fietsen," a short bicycle ride. This I did after dinner when I had finished my homework for the day. I also went on the weekends. I remember one evening in particular when I went for a ride on one of the roads where people walked a lot on weekends, not really a footpath but wider than that, though it was used for walking. My front wheel struck something, maybe a tree root, and both my bicycle and I went flying. The bike was all right, but I had a torn skirt and two bloody knees. I went a little farther and found a house, so I rang the bell and a lady opened the door.

Dag Mevrouw—Good evening Ma'am—I fell with my bike and hurt my knees. Could I please wash my knees before I go home?

Yes, of course, come right in, let's go into the kitchen.

And the lady gave me soap and a towel and even provided

two big bandaids. At that time, it was truly safe to do this kind of thing. So I washed up and then

Dank U wel, Mevrouw—thank you very much, Ma'am—that was very kind of you.

She never asked my name, nor did I ask hers, but it went without saying at that time that, if one rang the bell and asked for help, this help would be given. So the bike gave me more freedom than I had had before; it made it also very much easier to go and see friends because now I didn't need to take the streetcar any more.

When I was still fourteen, but already in the Amsterdams Lyceum, my parents decided that I ought to have dancing lessons, what we now call ballroom dancing. This was supposed to be a part of every well-brought-up young person. The arrangements were made and once they had been made, I was informed that from that moment on, every Tuesday night I would have to go. I protested loudly and long but nothing helped. I had to go. I had to take the streetcar to midtown and then walk about half a block to the dancing teacher's studio. I was frightened out of my mind the first time, since I had no idea what was going to be expected of me.

No, I don't want to go! I don't want to do this. Why do I have to learn to dance? It's not going to do any good. I'll be clumsy and everybody will laugh at me. This is so silly. I'd much rather stay home and read. I'd even rather do homework!

After the first time, I was no longer quite so frightened, but still scared enough. I had always known that I was not at all musical, that I couldn't carry a tune and that I couldn't hear the difference between tones unless they were very high or very low. Now I was supposed to follow a rhythm which I couldn't hear either. Of course, in the beginning all of us, boys and girls alike, were clumsy. But most of the others managed to remember the steps and could follow the music. I couldn't do either and I was always stepping on my partner's feet. I felt ashamed and embarrassed. This was supposed to be easy and fun. For me it wasn't either easy or fun. I hated the Tuesday nights and when the series of lessons was over and I heard that this would be celebrated with a "ball," I despaired completely. A long dress was necessary for this and my mother managed to borrow one, since I didn't have one and we couldn't yet afford to buy one. So that problem was out of the way. On the evening when the ball took place, the three of us, my parents and I, went to the hotel where this event was held. No one asked me to dance—as I had expected: naturally, why should they?—so I danced with my father a couple of times and we went home fairly early. However, if I thought that this "problem" was now taken care of, I was vastly mistaken.

The following February, the Amsterdams Lyceum celebrated its birthday with a festive evening, called Diës. We students were pretty much obliged to go. So I acquired an evening dress, my own this time, and went off to the lyceum. There was a band and there were refreshments and the students could dance to the music of the band. I didn't think anyone would ask me. Who would want his feet stepped on all the time, after all?

I might as well not have come. Nobody is going to ask me to dance and, anyway, even if someone did, I really don't dance well, so it would just be a disaster. I'm going to sit here and pretend to have a headache; that way nobody has to ask me and I can avoid the whole thing.

And so I did. I sat with my head in my hands; one or two people asked me what was the matter and I said that I had a headache. Since I was known to have headaches, nobody was surprised. Some people did ask why I didn't just go home then. For this I had, naturally, no answer; I did have the feeling that we had to stay till the end of the evening. Of course, that hadn't been an overt order, but since nobody left early, I suppose the other students had the same feeling. When the Diës was over, at midnight, I went home, firmly decided that this was the last Diës I would ever go to. It was one promise to myself which I kept.

⌒ *Bad Gastein*

As I mentioned before, at age fifteen I came down with rheumatoid arthritis. Nothing much could be done at that time, but I had to go to the doctor every week and get an injection of formic acid, which was supposed to help. I hated the injections, because I hated needles but there was nothing for it; I had to go. They didn't help and neither did the various ointments which I was given to put on the affected hand, which then was also bound up in a bandage so that the ointment would not stain my clothes. Pretty soon it became clear that my temporomandibular joint, the TMJ, the jaw joint just under the ear, was also affected. I could no longer open my mouth completely, going to the dentist became even more than normal torture, and I could also no longer bite into an apple or a raw carrot or anything else that was hard. The doctor recommended that I go to one of the health resorts which were known for help with arthritis. I could not, of course, go by myself, so my mother came with me. The first year we went to Baden near Zurich, in Switzerland. There was a swimming pool with warm, supposedly healing, water and every other day I had to submit to a mud bath of healing mud, called fango. I didn't see or feel any difference after the treatment, so the second year we went to Austria, to Bad Gastein, in the mountains. We went with another couple, friends of my parents, Mr. and Mrs. Katz. Bad Gastein has, unfortunately, a lot of rain so we had to spend a lot of time inside, rather than take walks. After the first few days, I began to notice that Mr. Katz seemed to like to touch me. He always had an arm around my shoulders, or a hand on my arm, and as time went on, this became more marked and more often.

I don't think that's right, somehow. I don't like him much, but I have to be polite. So I can't really say anything, can I? But I hate his touching me! He always takes me by the hand—and I am too old for that, really—or has a hand on my cheek or on my arm. Yuk! Maybe I should say something—but how can I and still be polite to him? What am I going to do?

Eventually I did what I should have done right away and went to my mother and told her about it. We shared a room, so this was easy. She wanted to know just exactly what was going on and I told her. Then she said she would speak to Mrs. Katz and that she, in her turn, would speak to Mr. Katz. My mother was as good as her word. She spoke to Mrs. Katz the next morn- ing and from that moment on, the touching stopped. I don't know what my mother said, nor do I know what Mrs. Katz said upon hearing this, but Mr. Katz left me alone thereafter. I did not understand at that time what he really wanted, nor did I un- derstand that until much later.

I must have been about sixteen or seventeen when this hap- pened and I had no idea that this could be called sexual harass- ment or abuse. I also had no idea that mothers don't always be- lieve their daughters when this subject comes up. It was natural for me to go to my mother and I thought that it was natural for my mother to "fix" the problem. I don't know how this in- fluenced the friendship between the Katzes and my parents and noone ever told me. The whole thing was simply not men- tioned again.

Much later, in other places, the same thing happened. Some men touched me in an inappropriate manner and in inap- propriate places, but I was older and was able to take care of it myself. Mostly these men were strangers. I had, equally, no idea that this happened in the family circle as well. In Bad Gastein, however, I was just glad that the problem had gone away. I avoided Mr. Katz as much as possible and was, under no circumstances, ever alone with him. That was also easy to do, since the four of us took our meals together and spent time together as a foursome. Some time was spent also with just my mother. We took walks when the weather allowed, or went to the village or did other things.

Bad Gastein didn't help the arthritis either, so the third year we went to Aix-les-Bains in France. This time, however, we went alone, my mother and I. In the chapter "Het Amsterdams Lyceum" I have already explained what happened there, that I could not speak French though I had studied the language for several years. Aix-les-Bains may have somewhat helped my French, but it didn't help the arthritis at all, so thereafter we did not go to any other health resort. The formic acid injections had also stopped by then and nothing further was done or even could be done. So after Aix-les-Bains, summer vacations were spent in other ways.

While we were in Aix-les-Bains, I tried to read Thomas Mann's *Zauberberg*—*The Magic Mountain*. I didn't really understand it and found the language very difficult as well. In the end I skipped the parts I didn't understand and read only the remainder. I did not find it very interesting at that time, but I've also not reread it. I had read other books by Mann and had understood those perfectly well, but this one was beyond me. At the end of my course of treatment, we went back home and I went back to the Amsterdams Lyceum.

The rheumatoid arthritis stayed for a while in my TMJ and my right hand. Eventually, it spread throughout my body, settling also in the other hand and various other places. Today, there are better treatments to help the swelling and the pain, but there is still no cure for it.

⌒ *England*

I graduated from the Amsterdams Lyceum in 1953. Since I had
changed from the classical department in the lyceum to the
modern department, I had not had the requisite background to
study pharmacy in Holland. But, as of the year before, my father had commuted from Amsterdam to London, England every week. My uncle Henry, my father's brother, had fallen seriously ill and my father had had to take over my uncle's business
and take care of it as well as of his own. He therefore commuted
to and from London, spending the week in London and the
weekend at home in Amsterdam. He had friends in London and
one of these suggested that it might be a good idea if I came to
London as well. I could then go to a tutoring school and be tutored in the appropriate subjects, such as physics, chemistry,
and the like, and, of course, English. Once I had taken the exams in London, I could then go to university in England.
I would live with an English family who lived a little outside
of London and who took in boarders. We talked it over, my
parents and I, and we decided that it would probably be a good
idea. At the same time that I would be tutored in English,
I would be speaking it every day, all the time with everybody. So
it was then, that after the summer holidays of 1953, I went off to
England. Yet another separation. Yet another place to live. Yet

another language. Yet another leaving behind of treasured people and things. But there was nothing else to do; I did not know
what else to do since I could not study pharmacy in Holland.

The family turned out to be very nice; there were father,
mother, and three daughters, of whom two no longer lived at
home. The youngest was still there and, besides me, there was
another boarder as well. My English improved very rapidly although there were problems here and there. I did not, of
course, know all the exact expressions and words for everything
and some sentences came out rather strangely. The father of
the family taught us boarders to call him "Sir" and so we did.
He was a teacher in a private school for boys and they called
him "Sir," so we did too. Later, when I met other people and
called the men "Sir," I found out that they did not like that at
all, because it made them feel old or at least older. It betokened
a respect that they didn't feel was earned. In addition, when nobody was home, I had to answer the telephone and mostly did
not understand the messages or the name of whoever called.
Indeed, this is one of the more difficult things in learning a new
language. Once, the telephone rang again and I answered it. I
understood right away that it was one of the older daughters of
the family where I lived. But…I could not for the life of me understand the message the young woman wanted to leave for her
parents, nor did I understand the number she gave me where
they could ring her back. She must have repeated the number
five or six times with great patience. In the end, though, she just
said to tell her parents that she would call again later. I felt very
ashamed that I could not understand the number, but did not
know what to do about it. I got along reasonably well with the
family and the other boarder. The rest was not so easy. I was
tutored in chemistry, physics, and English. I did very well in the
latter, writing compositions in English with not too many mistakes. Over time, there were fewer and fewer mistakes and my
grades improved. I began to read in English as well. It was very
hard in the beginning and I had a fat dictionary next to me
where I could look up words. Naturally, this did not make for

easy or fast reading. Eventually somebody (I no longer remember who) suggested that I read in English something like a detective novel which I had already read in another language. This would have the advantage that I already knew the story and the language in a detective novel would be, more or less, normal, every day language. I did this and it worked perfectly. My English, from then on, improved by leaps and bounds.

Chemistry was not too bad and I enjoyed it though I had to work harder at it than at English. It had its own little pitfalls, though. There was one evening when I was to meet my father and some friends of his for dinner. Naturally, that would have to be the day when a test tube broke in my hand and both my hands were brown with iodine. I could not get it off and was forced to meet my father and his friends with brown-tinted hands. On the whole, though, I had no problems with chemistry. But physics! Physics was a disaster! I remember one morning when my tutor explained the pulley to me. He explained very slowly and clearly, asking me at every opportunity whether I understood.

Do you understand this part?
Yes, I do.
Tell me how it works.
Well, it works like this

and I would tell him with his own words exactly what he had said and wanted to hear. But then...then he changed the numbers. And I was hopelessly lost. It was as though he had explained that seven and three make ten. Then he asked that I put together six and four. And, of course, I could not do it. I could only sit there and look at him, no doubt rather sheepishly and without any idea at all what I was supposed to do. After several months of this, we decided that it really was totally hopeless and from then on my tutor gave me books to read in English and we spent the tutoring hour discussing them. He introduced me to John Steinbeck, Ernest Hemingway, Somerset Maugham, and others.

Needless to say, I never did take my exams in physics, and

since I needed it as well as chemistry for pharmacy, there was no sense in taking my chemistry exam. I did, however, take my English exam which I passed with flying colors.

So, on one weekend when all three of us were home, the family got together again and the three of us came to the conclusion that, obviously, pharmacy was not meant for me nor I for it. But, perhaps, since I liked children, I would make a good kindergarten teacher. So my parents inquired where one could be trained; it turned out that there were special schools for this. We then went for an interview. Chemistry and physics were not needed, but what was needed I didn't have either. I would have needed to study enough music for kindergarten purposes, for singing songs to the children and for teaching them songs. Unfortunately, I am tone-deaf and cannot carry a tune. Already in second grade I had been told by my then teacher that I could do whatever I wanted, just please don't sing. So kindergarten teacher was out also.

Finally we came to the conclusion that what I was best at was languages. I didn't really know what profession one could have with the study of languages, but it *was* what I was best at. After more inquiries and letters, we decided that it would be a good idea to go to the university of Geneva, Switzerland. Attached to the university was the International Interpreters' School where we would be taught translation, consecutive interpretation, and simultaneous interpretation, as well as some law, geography, and other things of each country where the language we studied was spoken. So, just before the new fall semester began, I went off to Geneva and tried to settle in.

⌒ *Geneva*

I had not really made any friends in England, but I was, by now, fluent in the language. So I made my goodbyes, from my various teachers, but especially from my physics/literature teacher. I said goodbye to the family where I had lived for that time. More uprooting. More separation. Yet another place to live with yet another language, French in this case, since Geneva is in the French part of Switzerland. I had not put down any roots in England; the roots I had had in Holland had been broken. I could not put down roots in Geneva. I lived in the "Maison des Etudiants," the Students' House where people of all nationalities lived in private rooms. We all had our meals together, then took coffee all together in the living room. The "overseer," the lady who was in charge of us, was a rather unpleasant person, but the students were nice and very varied. I made friends with an Egyptian girl, an Italian girl, a Portuguese young woman, various Dutch girls, a couple of Greek young men and many others. Of course, only French was spoken, both during dinner and during the coffee hour. In any event, French was what most of us had in common, albeit that our French was by no means perfect. The studies were interesting as well; we were obliged to take two languages besides French, which was, of course, the "native" language. Eventually I had to unlearn Genevan expressions and replace them all with "proper" French. Never-theless, French was the language spoken in Geneva and so our principal language, no matter what else we studied. For the other two languages, I chose English and German. After one had completed the course of study, which took about two years, and one had finished and passed both the written and the oral exams for each language, one could choose yet another language to complement the earlier ones and receive a second "complementary" diploma. This I did for the third year and chose Dutch. After finishing that course of study, there were more exams to pass. They weren't just exams of language as such, though of course that was in it as well: translations from French into the other language and from the other language into French, as well as a long composition in the language we had studied. In addition, one was also examined on the geography and the law of the country, the culture and anything else which had to do with the country whose language one had studied.

In between courses and classes, though, we also had time to explore Geneva and its surroundings. Geneva is a pretty city, with a lovely old part, called "La vieille ville"—the old town—and it had all sorts of small, winding streets, little shops and restaurants, old churches and museums. In the downtown area, the modern area, there were the bigger shops, department stores and hotels. Lake Geneva is truly beautiful and water sports are in great favor. Unfortunately we found that the people of Geneva were not nearly as attractive as their city. They were too fond of money and therefore, since none of us had all that much money, considered all students poor, unable to spend money and therefore of no concern. As a result, they were mostly rather surly to us and none too polite. In addition, our French was not always perfect and the Genevans looked down their noses at us. In time we learned French, of course, but the interesting thing to me was that the French language spoken in France is much more beautiful than the Genevan French. Genevan French is spoken with rather a sing-song accent and it has words which don't exist in the French of France. The Genevans use words, expressions and numbers in their own way which occasionally results in French, which the French think is incorrect. In reality, it is simply "Genevan French." The French of France, in their turn, look down their noses at the Genevans who speak Genevan French.

In the beginning of my stay in Geneva, I also had a harrowing experience. I had gone out with a group of students to a café where we later often had coffee. Everyone was talking, as best we could, to everyone. Then, the girl sitting next to me said, seemingly all of a sudden and with no context that I had heard:

I don't like Jews. I always know when I'm near one; I can just tell. They are so disagreeable and they smell. I don't know how I can tell, but I can—I always know right away.

Had I been older and more experienced, perhaps I would have said something. As it was, though I knew that she very obviously could *not* tell that I was Jewish, I said nothing. I did not want a quarrel, I did not want any kind of altercation and, mostly, I did not want to attract attention (I had learned that lesson very well!). So I remained silent. I did, however, avoid this girl from then on.

One of the friends I made in Geneva turned out to be a lifelong friend. She is the above-mentioned Portuguese young woman, named Elisa. She came originally from Oporto, but lived in Lisbon with her husband when I first met her. She spoke fluent French already when she came and helped me a great deal in the beginning. We both had rooms in the Maison des Etudiants and met there. We took several classes together, studied together and passed the exams together. We also explored the surroundings together. Students were supposed to spend time in those countries of which they studied the language. That was as good an excuse as any to spend some vacation time in Paris, France. Elisa went to meet her husband, who studied in France; I went to see Paris. We went to the theater together, saw a number of museums, experimented with restaurants, looked at a lot of stained glass windows in churches and

I fell in love with gargoyles. They serve as decoration on many churches but also have a practical purpose: they are the beginning of many downspouts where the rainwater can run off the roofs. I found them exotic, individual and fascinating—at that, I still do. We wandered through the old part of Paris, went to the fleamarkets and, on the whole, had a wonderful time. I began to write again in Paris, short stories mostly, but not this time about Jewish girls who had experienced the war. These stories were in the form of fairy tales and it wasn't till many years after I had come to the USA that I reread them and found that they had, indeed, different characters, but that they all spoke of the same theme: loneliness, aloneness, being different, not fitting in. I didn't see that at the time, but I needed to write them and so I did. Much later, as of 1985, I began to write poetry, but during my study time I was not able to do that. It was yet another thing that I had not really learned to do and had to find out on my own. In school we learned to write in proper sentences and paragraphs, of course, and to discuss a theme from the beginning through a middle and finally to the end. But we did not learn to write stories. That, I had to just find out while doing it.

After three years, my studies in Geneva were over; I had passed my exams and received my diplomas (the Interpreters' School gave no degrees, only diplomas): one for the first three languages and one for the complementary language. I was now a full-fledged translator. With my diplomas in hand, I returned to Holland and looked for a job.

The time in London and Geneva had taught me many things besides English and French. But I still felt that I did not fit in with the others who were there, I still felt very much alone, I still felt that I could not and should not speak about what had happened to me as a child. Camp stories did not fit into the Interpreters' School. Neither did stories of wearing the yellow star. So I remained closed-up and introverted and tried to get by as best I could. In 1985, I wrote a poem on "belonging" which, with very few and minor alterations, could as easily have been written in Geneva. I add it here.

BELONGING

Belonging is sharing a background of traditions,
a spiritual likeness to those around you,
fitting in.
I don't belong here, and yet I do.

Belonging is feeling at home,
understanding and being understood,
being like the others.
I don't belong here, and yet I do.

Belonging is playing the same childhood games,
singing the same childhood songs,
reading the same childhood tales.
I did not play those games,
sing those songs or read those tales.
I don't feel that I belong.

Belonging is celebrating the same holidays,
knowing the meaning of them,
feeling deep-down why they exist.
I do not feel that meaning inside of me.
I do not feel that I belong.

Belonging is sharing the same experiences,
knowing that *this* place is *mine*.
But I have more than one place.
How can I belong when all are mine,
yet none is?

Belonging is speaking the same language,
knowing the words as well as the gestures.
But I have more than one language.
How can I belong when all are mine,
yet none is?

Belonging is being part of a group,
keeping your "self" in that group,
yet being part of it so that you know
that these are *your* people,
so that you feel whole when you are with them.
I don't really feel whole with any group,
yet sometimes I feel whole with some.
Will I ever belong?

I was born in one country,
I grew up in a second,
I live in a third.
My birth country rejected me, then;
Now I deny it.
The second and third are mine, though,
yet neither is, wholly.
I belong to both,
yet I belong to neither.
Will I ever belong?

I am torn between two continents,
both home,
yet neither is, wholly.
I belong to both,
yet I belong to neither.
Will I ever belong?

I could have written these words in London. I could have written them in Geneva. At that time, I didn't divide my time between two continents, was not "torn between" them. Yet the feelings expressed in this poem were true also in England and in Switzerland. Those feelings are still true, even though I have, by now, lived in this country for over forty years. They are not likely to ever change. I will always be a foreigner, always be different, never belong totally.

☞ *Return to Amsterdam*

Having finished my studies in Geneva, I returned to Amsterdam with my two translator's diplomas. My parents had moved to London completely by then, so that my father could continue his and his brother's business from there. I, however, could not go to London to find a job. In order to work in England, I would have needed, first: a job, second: a working permit for that job. It had, moreover, to be a job which no English person could do or else they would hire an English person and not a foreigner. Since I had to have a job to get a working permit and a working permit to get a job, this was obviously impossible. In Amsterdam, I could easily find work; I was a Dutch citizen and as such needed no permits or anything else. I just needed some company to hire me.

To begin with, I moved in with the couple, Mr. and Mrs. Van der Guus, who took care of our apartment and my father's business in Amsterdam, and started job hunting. I was now a translator but had no experience. Still I found a job with a medical publisher who brought out a monthly journal with extracts of medical articles of all kinds, translated into English from their original language. I earned very little but liked the work. Together with translating, we girls who worked in that department also had to proofread the various articles, which gave rise to much laughter when the translation was, occasionally, bizarre. I remember clearly an article that mentioned premature babies, born in the tenth month. We asked the various doctors working at the same publisher what that was likely to mean, but it took us weeks to get an answer, which then showed that by "tenth month" was meant the tenth month of the year, namely October. I made some casual friends at that office but saw the people mostly in the office and not in after-office-hours.

I didn't really want to stay with the Van der Guuses, because neither they nor I had any real privacy. So several months later, I found a room I could rent, in a house where another young woman from my office also lived. So, I moved out of the apartment. In addition, I had entered, now, finally, in my mid-twenties, the rebellious stage which I had not had in my teens.

The room I rented made me more independent. It also made me poorer because the rent ate up a large part of my already small salary. It was one big room, with a balcony. It had a table, a bed, some chairs, and a very small electric stove with two burners. Because it was located in the northeast of the house, it was bitterly cold in winter. But heating cost money, so, in order to stay warm, I mostly sat with blankets wrapped around me or went to bed. Towards the end of the month, when money was really short, I would take back the milk bottles for which I had had to pay a deposit and which I had kept the whole month. The deposit money which was returned to me served to keep me fed for the last days of the month. At that time, we had only glass bottles, paid a deposit on every bottle, and gave them back to the store to get our deposit back.

When my father came to Amsterdam from London, as he did about once a month, to take care of the Dutch part of his business, he took one look at the room, knew that I barely made it through the month financially, and gave me an envelope with a month's room rent and food money in it.

Papi, I don't want that! I have a job, I'm earning my own money and I need no longer be dependent on you! I can manage to pay for the room and for my food. Really, I don't want it. I don't need it!

My father did not want to listen. He more or less forced me to take the envelope. But he had not counted on the fact that I was just as stubborn as he.

I'm not going to use this. I'll put it away in a safe spot and I will live on what I make. I will. Now, where shall I put it? Aahh, that's a good spot, there in that drawer. I won't even have to see it there.

The next month, when my father came again to Amsterdam, I handed him his envelope back, unopened, and the subject of money or my needing or wanting it never came up again. He was upset that I gave him back the envelope untouched—but I had been upset that he had given it to me. *"So,"* I figured, *"we're even."*

The young woman who lived in the same house as I did and I became friendlier and I also made another friend, Jaap, who worked in the office as well. We met one morning by chance while I was walking from home to the office as was he, so we walked together. Thereafter we made it a point to meet and walk the rest of the way together. We spent some time together as well, had some good conversations and altogether became good friends.

When I could, I visited my parents in London. There, they had a furnished apartment in a big Victorian house which had been split up into apartments. Ours was on the ground floor. It was never my parents' intention to move to London permanently, so they had not brought over their own furniture, but had rented this apartment instead. Still, they remained in London from 1953 until 1960. At that time, my father was able to sell his business and they moved to Zurich, Switzerland, where they lived the rest of their lives. They chose Zurich because in Zurich German is spoken and my father wanted to audit courses at the University. He spoke Dutch, of course, but German was his first language and he felt more at home with it and more comfortable.

When my father came over from London to Amsterdam, occasionally my mother would come with him. On various holiday occasions I went over to London to visit them. On one of those occasions, the car in which I was a passenger was involved in an accident and I ended up in the hospital with what was then called a broken neck. I stayed there several days and had a stiff collar round my neck so as not to move it. My mother came to visit and to bring me some things I needed. She took one look at me and said, to the horror of the nearby nurse, "A broken neck? I thought you died of that!" I laughed; it was a typical my-mother remark, but the nurse thought that remark very unkind. Eventually I was allowed to go home, still with my collar. I stayed in London for probably about six weeks before the collar came off. After that I went back to work in Amsterdam. My friendships with Jaap and Dina (the young woman with whom I worked) flourished, but, as I look back, I don't see any major emotional investment. It was, somehow, a rather superficial friendship, in spite of the late night conversations with Dina or the long walks with conversation with Jaap. Looking back from this long distance, I think that I was not at all ready to have any deep friendships. The lesson learned in my childhood was too well learned: don't get close to anybody—because if you do, you will lose that person. Lose that person as I lost Hans and other childhood friends. Lose them as I lost my grandparents and great-aunts and -uncles and their descendants. Lose them as I lost my pre-war parents. True, I had the same parents after the war as before the war, but the war had irrevocably changed them. So I never did get close to either Dina or Jaap.

To the United States of America

In 1958, friends of my parents, the same Fred and Jetty Benjamin whom I have mentioned before and who lived in the United States, invited me to come and visit and to see how I liked it here. I had been unable to find work in England because of the already stated reasons. So in 1959, I handed in my resignation at work in Amsterdam and took a plane to the United States. In those days it was still a propeller plane and it took many, many hours of flight before arrival. I arrived in New York, dressed warmly in my thickest winter coat. From New York I took another plane to California, where Fred and Jetty lived. Arriving in February in California, I found typical California weather: warm (at that time still "very hot" to me) and sunny. My coat was too heavy and I didn't need the shawl around my neck, nor the gloves which I had on. Sunbathing in February—who had ever heard of that? Unbelievable! Fantastic! But true!

I spent some time doing nothing, then decided I would like to go to college. I applied to UCLA—the University of California, Los Angeles—and was accepted and even given a year of credit for the work at the University of Geneva. Again, as in Geneva, I studied languages, making French my major. I figured that nobody would be interested in learning Dutch (after all, what for?) and that there were many Americans who would be far better than I at teaching English. I did not want to teach German. So that left French. Once I had been accepted, I moved into a dormitory. I hoped to make some friends there, as well as through my classes, but that hope was not really fulfilled. In hindsight I think that I was too reserved and not really able to open up to people. At the time I only felt—once again—the odd one out. My English was reasonably fluent, but, of course, I had an accent and people were always asking where I came from. I did not fit in in other ways as well, being, still, far too European. In my second semester, I had a terrifying experience. At that time, air alarms were tested at ten o'clock in the morning, every last Friday of the month, a fact nobody had told me, presumably because everyone thought I knew it. As I was walking from one class to another on campus, suddenly the alarms went off. I had no time to think, something in me took over and I raced, as fast as I could, to the nearest shelter I knew: the library which had restrooms in the basement. I ran down the stairs, ran into the restrooms and cowered there, shivering and shaking, for a good twenty minutes, trying to talk myself into truly believing that this was *not* an air attack, *not* a bomb attack, that, in fact, nothing was wrong at all and that it was no longer 1941 or 1943 but 1960 and that the war was over. Over? Apparently not, at least not for me. I missed class that day—but it didn't occur to me that I needed help. I thought that this was an isolated incident, that I would not react that way again and that everything was all right. In any event: what sort of help? In Europe, at that time, when people went to a psychologist or psychiatrist, it was "because they were crazy." I knew *I* was not crazy, I had just had a scare, nothing else. It was nothing. I could handle it. I didn't tell anybody but told myself that I was fine, I had adjusted very well.

I'm fine, I'm very well adjusted. I don't need anybody. Anyway, where would I go for help? No, no, don't even think about it, you don't need "help." (I addressed myself as "you.") *Nobody wants to hear about what happened. It's bad enough that you're not from here, that you're different, don't make it worse. You can't really say what you want to say anyway. It's just not a problem. It'll go away, especially if you don't think about it. After all, you're not crazy, not even a little bit. Leave it all alone, there's nothing anybody can do about it.*

"It" being the past, of course. At that time, nobody asked any questions, nobody wanted to hear what had happened to us in Europe and we, the survivors, were in no way able to speak about it. I never considered myself a "survivor" or a "victim"; those were not words used at the time. The war had happened and it had been bad, but now it was all over. Don't think about it; it'll go away. That wasn't just my thought; it was a general thought, at least among the people I knew. It certainly had been that way in my family and in the small community of Jews whom we, my family and I, knew.

Sometime during the three years I needed to receive my B.A., I decided to remain permanently in the United States. I didn't think about why I wanted to stay here. I felt freer, more at ease than in Europe. It almost seemed as though I could breathe more easily. I could be more independent here. Many years later, it occurred to me that I had wanted to stay because here in the United States, there were no ghosts. Of course, by then, my ghosts had followed me, had found the key to my secret drawer, and had unlocked it. But that was much later. For now, I set about getting my green card and the various needed papers. Then I received my B.A. in French, with a minor in German. If I wanted to teach—which I did—I also needed an M.A. So my studies continued. Though I felt at ease in the United States, I also still felt "other." I figured that was because I was an immigrant, had been brought up differently, had different customs and manners and, of course, the accent. It was because of the accent that I was told not to teach Elementary School because the children would pick up my accent and that was not good. Instead I studied for a credential for teaching in what was then called a Junior College, now a Community College.

My mother and father, 1968.

My mother, myself, and my father, mid-1970s.

☞ My First Job

The summer after the semester in which I received my B.A. I spent in the "French House." In actual fact, this was the same dorm in which I lived during the school year, but it now held only students of French, students of all levels. Only French was to be spoken; we had discussions at mealtimes and put on a play as well, all in French. During that summer, one of my teachers suggested that I should apply for the post of Teaching Assistant, since I was going to earn my M.A. in French. That sounded good and I applied and, to my great surprise, was accepted. So now I had a job and could actually earn some money. Like my job in Amsterdam, this one didn't pay very much either; my mother said: "Too little to live on and too much to die on." Truer word was never spoken—but the teaching experience was enormously valuable. We had one regular daily class to teach, beginning, usually, with a beginner's level of French. In the second semester, we taught a second semester French class, a third semester French class in our third semester, and so on. In addition we taught a conversation class twice a week and worked in the language laboratory, listening to students and correcting them as they did their oral work. In between all that, we studied for our own courses and for the rapidly approaching Master exams. Two years seemed a long time, but the exams loomed very quickly.

After earning my M.A., I now needed a "real" job, one in which I could actually earn enough to live on. One of my teacher friends told me that UCLA had a sort of registry where one could register and would then be called if and when a job was available. I did that and was called almost immediately. As I said before, my major was French and my minor German. This particular job, which was at Pasadena City College (also known as PCC) for a long-term substitute, was actually for a German major and a French minor. Yet I went and applied and, to my joy, got the job, which, so they told me, would continue after the first semester as a full-time post. I went to a job interview, very frightened because I had never done this before, and was told that I would have to speak with one teacher in French and with another in German so that they could hear how good (or bad) my languages were. After that the head of the department spoke with me for a while and I pointed out that I was an immigrant and a Jew, thinking that if they didn't want me for either reason, then they had an out and I would not get a job only to be fired later. What I didn't know until much later was that the head of the department was himself an immigrant and a Jew and, as was I, a Holocaust survivor. I soon found out that the fact that I was an immigrant made no difference at all: most of my new colleagues were immigrants also. Many varied accents floated through the department and all of us laughed at the many varied mistakes in English we all managed to make. All of us spoke, besides English, at least two other languages, and sometimes more. It was a very good school and a very good department and my new colleagues were easy to get along with.

Again, though, I made no close friends among them. In part that was on purpose since I didn't want to work all day with the same people with whom I would then be friends after school. I did not think that a very good idea—a bit limiting. In part it was also because my social skills—as we now say—were very poor. Since my parents were so introverted after the war, I grew up the same way; I never made friends easily. If one is not taught social skills at home, where does one learn them? I found that I had not learned them. Then there was also the fact that I did not grow up in the United States and therefore did not have the same childhood experiences, games, television and radio programs as people who did grow up here. All of that, and probably other factors as well, kept me from making close friends. I did, eventually, make close friends with one of my colleagues but it took many years. It did not then occur to me that, if I wanted friends, I would have to go out and make them. That they would not come to me. That insight did not come till much later. There were no more scares such as the alarm scare at UCLA. If, at PCC, we had a fire alarm or an earthquake alarm, we teachers knew this beforehand and we were told where to go and what to do, where to lead our students and what to have with us. Those alarms, then, did not come as a surprise and, though they left me very uneasy, I thought nothing of it. In hindsight, the first scare should have alerted me that something, to put it mildly, was not quite right. The fact that I was uneasy after announced fire or earthquake alarms should have done the same. But, as I had so well been taught in my childhood, I pushed it all away, packed it all into a drawer, locked the drawer tightly and threw the key away. Meanwhile I kept reassuring myself that I was fine, I had adjusted beautifully, after all I had "only" been in Theresienstadt, which was, so the Germans said, a camp for privileged people. So nothing so terrible had happened to me; others had had it far worse. And that was that, for a long time.

I enjoyed teaching and I enjoyed my students. I found out that I was, in fact, a good teacher. That made me feel good because it was something that I had accomplished. It was not something that I had inherited or that I had been given by someone. I also found out that I was not—and still am not—a committee person. We teachers had to be part of various committees and, as much as I could, I avoided that. I could not avoid it completely, but to a great extent I could and did. On the whole, though, I was very happy in my chosen field.

⌒ The In Between Years

For many years, things went along this way. I remained "numb," in the sense that I did not think about the war years. There was, in my opinion, no sense in thinking about them because I could not talk about them, so why bring it all up, even to myself? Thinking about it would just give me a migraine or possibly bad dreams. Not nightmares yet, but dreams from which I would awaken with a shock, though I would not be able to remember just what the dream had been about. In addition to that, the adult survivors I knew, i.e. those who were already adult when the war started, did not believe anything I said in any event. On the few occasions that, for example, Jetty brought up something about the camps, a conversation much like the following would take place. Jetty might say something about the mud in Westerbork:

Everything always turned to mud when it rained. Remember the "main street"? It was a river of mud any time it rained.

Jetty, do you remember this from Westerbork? When the trains left, the commandant would have his dog with him at the rail line. He had it with him also when he walked through the camp. I used to be afraid of that dog. It was a German shepherd. I would try and hide in the barracks because I never knew what he was going to do or whether the dog would attack.

No, no, that can't be right; I never saw a dog. I'm sure there was no dog; I know that I would have seen it. You were only a child, how could you possibly remember such a thing? You would not have been afraid either because you were only a child. You used to like dogs. You're imagining it. There was no dog when we were transported out.

I heard this kind of thing from Jetty all the time. I didn't know many adult survivors at that time, but my parents had occasionally said the same thing. Much later, the first time I went to a Survivors' Gathering, I again heard the same thing from others who had been adults during the war years. As long as I had been "only" a child, I could not have suffered, I could not now remember, I could not have understood what had happened, I had surely imagined it all. In approximately 1998—when I was 65 years old—an adult survivor friend told me:

You don't know that. You can't possibly remember that—you were only a child. You didn't understand. You seemed quite self-sufficient; you went here and there by yourself. Anyway, you can't know that; you are only a child.

"*Are*" not "*were*." These sorts of conversations and expressions devalued my memories so thoroughly that for too many years afterwards I thought many things, like the dog, were my imagination and couldn't have happened. As for the dog, in the late 1980's, I went to Holland and to the Netherlands Institute of War Documentation in Amsterdam. There, in their boxes full of photographs of Westerbork, I found a photograph showing the Westerbork commandant with his dog. I felt as though I had been given back a piece of myself. So...to whom would I have talked, even if I had wanted to? If I had been able to? Who would have listened? By then, my parents had died so I could not ask them. Was there anyone else? I didn't think so. Not to my knowledge, anyway.

At that time I also thought that, quite possibly, even probably, I was the only child to have survived as a child. I did not know any other Child Survivors. Because of that, I thought that my reactions to various things were silly, even absurd. I did not know anyone else who, going into a restaurant, or other public building, immediately looked for a second exit. I did not know anyone else who cringed, hearing sirens. I did not know anyone else who, standing in a foodline, like in a cafeteria, became uneasy. I did not know anyone else who, automatically, had great quantities of soap and toilet paper in the house; who felt jittery when that was not the case. I thought that, perhaps, I was crazy, after all. At the very least, I thought that I was not "normal."

However, I enjoyed PCC, I loved teaching (I still do), I thoroughly enjoyed both my colleagues and my students. I managed to buy a house and enjoyed that. It had a small back and front yard and I began to plant flowers and plants and enjoyed working in the garden. During summer vacations I travelled to Europe to see my parents. When anybody asked me what I was doing in summer, I would say: *I'm going home to visit my parents.*

Of course, I also said: *I'm going home, back to California*, at the end of my stay. In reality, I was "home" neither in Europe, nor in California. Immigrants tend to "sit on the fence" as one of my cousins once said, and I certainly did. Today, after forty-three years in California, there are still times when I feel European rather than American and there are times in Europe when I feel American rather than European. I no longer belong in Europe. I will never totally belong in America.

In 1978, the miniseries "Holocaust" was shown on TV. I watched it, like everybody else, but had no reaction to it other than that it was too sanitized.

We didn't look like that. We were too thin, we were dirtier than the TV characters. The dirt was visible on us. We had no soap or very little and could not wash. The water was turned off very often, so the soap would not have helped anyway. We smelled. Our clothes were old and in rags and dirty. We could not get new clothes. With luck we acquired clothing from someone who had died. Theresienstadt (where part of "Holocaust" took place) was overcrowded; you couldn't ever walk in the street without bumping people. There were people everywhere. They sat in the streets, lay in the streets, slept in the streets, died in the streets. None of that is being shown in the movie. The rooms were dirty, dusty, even muddy after rain. There was far too little food. We were starving, seriously underweight. If we had had conditions like the ones shown, we would have thought that we were in Paradise!

It was my first experience with a sanitized and cleaned-up Holocaust. It was not to be my last. However, in that time, not even the TV series "Holocaust" stirred anything in me. It did in various other people, but I could not understand that. To me, it was just a sort of "cleaned up" picture which did not show the real truth as I had seen and known it. It was a movie entitled "Holocaust," but it wasn't our inmate-truth. It was a made-up town with actors, whereas we had been real inmates. There was no comparison to the real thing.

In 1983, I retired from PCC, but was called back the next year as a substitute for the rest of the year, then retired again in 1984. Towards the end of that year, I began having trouble with the past and began to think again that, surely this time, I was going crazy, that I was not "normal."

∽ *Trouble*

Towards the end of 1984, I began having what I then called "picture memories." They were not true memories, in that one can call up a memory in one's mind and look at it and then dismiss it. It's like looking at a photograph, a still picture. What happened to me, though, was different. It was a memory, yes, but I didn't call it up on purpose, I didn't look "at" it and it wasn't a still picture. Instead these (moving) pictures came unexpectedly at any time and I was in them. One that came very frequently in the beginning was a picture of Westerbork. I saw the barracks, saw the sandy road, the mud in the rain and saw myself, ten years old, running as fast as I could from something. I felt frightened. The "something" of which I was frightened was never visible. The running in the "picture memory" left me breathless in reality. I also felt frightened in reality. It was more than a memory, it was a re-happening. Later I learned that these things were called "flashbacks." There were few of them at first, but they became more frequent and more frightening. I relived a number of other scenes in both Westerbork and Theresienstadt. I had no idea what to do about it, but began to think I should ask my physician for a reference to a psychologist. That thought became more firmly fixed at each appearance of a "picture memory." I finally began to think seriously of trying to find help. It was then that various things started happening at once. I was taking classes at California State University, Fullerton and was told that there would be a meeting of a historical society where a psychologist would be speaking about adult survivors. So I went to that meeting. Theresienstadt was mentioned. After the meeting I went and introduced myself and said that I had been there also, but as a child. The psychologist gave me a telephone number to call; I spoke to another psychologist and, for a while, that was all. In the beginning of 1985—forty years after war's end—the first psychologist called me and wondered whether I would be interested in joining a discussion group, led by her and the second psychologist whom I had called. I jumped at the chance and when I went the first time, I found out that this group consisted solely of Child Survivors. Like me, they had each thought that they were the war's only surviving child. Some were, like me, camp survivors, others had been in hiding during part or all of the war. In spite of our different experiences, I found that the main experience was the same for us all: a sense of loss, of abandonment, of having memories which the grown-ups didn't validate and, in many cases, didn't believe. We were, after all, *only* children. Then, when we started talking in more detail and the psychologists started asking questions, I said that I had been "only" in Theresienstadt (not in any of the worse camps), and I was corrected. For the first time in my life, someone told me that there was no question of "only." Theresienstadt was very bad, as bad as any of the others, no matter what the propaganda about it said (indeed it was bad—only one-third of the inmates survived and of the 15,000 children under the age of 15 who were there at one time or another, only about 125 survived). For the first time in my life, my memories were taken seriously. If I remembered a dog in Westerbork, then a dog there had been. It was a revelation!

Shortly after the beginning of that discussion group, somebody, who is now a friend, called me up and invited me to a Child Survivors' meeting. I went and that was another revelation: here were many Child Survivors, children just like me, some younger, some older, who had been in camps, had been in hiding, had passed as Christians or had wandered about in forests. For some of them, more than one of these situations had been true. It was like a miracle to see so many Child Survivors in one room and know that they all had lived, in some way, through the Holocaust. From then on, I went to the meetings regularly and became very active in this group which is called "Child Survivors of the Holocaust, Los Angeles." I had had no idea that there were so many children who had survived. Our experiences were, of course, different in detail but yet so closely related that we could easily talk to each other and understand each other and our experiences. The group had been formed in mid-1983 and we bonded very, very quickly.

The original group was founded in Los Angeles, in 1983, by just a few people who came together at the invitation of one of the psychologists of the discussion group. They told me that they knew immediately that they wanted to meet again. So they did and, by word of mouth, the group grew. When I first became a member, there were maybe 150 of us. Today there are, in greater Los Angeles alone, over 400 members. We had—and have—all sorts of activities, some meant to be just fun and some meant to be helpful to each other. We are both a support group and a family group, the siblings which so many of us either lost in the Holocaust or never had. We could—and can—talk about our past and we know we will not be laughed at, nobody will say that we were "only" children, nobody will say that we cannot possibly remember or that we cannot know. And, perhaps best of all, we didn't need to explain things in detail. As the Dutch say, these fellow Child Survivors heard with "half an ear" and understood. As time passed, other groups came together in other states of the USA, so that today (in 2002) there is a Child Survivors' group in practically every state in the USA; there are Child Survivors' groups in Belgium, France, Holland, England, the Czech Republic, Poland and other European countries, in Canada, in Israel, in Latin America, in South Africa and in Australia.

In 1988 we had our first international get-together, where about 125 Child Survivors showed up. We have had—and are still having—an International Child Survivors' Conference since then, every year, in various places and countries. Today, the usual attendance is between 300 and 400 people, coming from all over the world.

The discussion group I had joined eventually ended after eight weeks and I knew that eight weeks had not been enough. All the stored-up anger, pain and sadness could not be talked out in eight weeks. Therefore I went into therapy which turned out to last five years, after which I, as one of my friends calls it, "graduated." Does that mean that, now, it's all out of my head and forgotten? Well…, no. What it does mean, however, is that I no longer think that I might be going crazy when I have a vision or a reaction to something. Are my ghosts gone? Well…, no. They are still around; they will always be with me. But they are no longer enemies to be shut away in a drawer with the key thrown away.

My mother, 1976,
age sixty-seven.

My father, 1977,
age seventy-three.

⤳ *The Later Years*

"The later years"—what does that mean? Are they the later years of the war? Or of my life? Actually the "later years" are now. They are the present, although they are also the past. One of my somewhat distant cousins said to me one time: *It's time to lay the ghosts.* She was, of course, right. There's only one problem: the ghosts will not lie down or go away. They'll always be there and they pop out at inconvenient and unpredictable times. They look over my shoulder and are always with me. They step forward and say: *Stop and look at me; I'm here.* They keep coming back when you least expect it and attack when you can least defend yourself. It's not a matter of laying the ghosts; it's a matter of learning how to live with them. The past intrudes all the time. I have already given a number of examples of that; here's an example of something that happened when a friend and I were going to visit the cousin in question. We were in the railroad station in London, England. Normally one can go to one's platform and wait there; this time the travelers were told to wait in front of a closed door. A space had been roped off and we were to wait behind that rope. I began to feel uneasy; it was a strange situation. Nobody knew why things were different that day. All of a sudden, a man in a uniform appeared—not a soldier's uniform, but another type, I don't know whether police or something else. As part of the uniform, this man wore high, black boots. I began to tremble but still didn't know what was going on. Then I saw that this man in uniform also had a dog on a leash, a German shepherd. At that moment, I "freaked out," I couldn't go anywhere, there was no place to run, I could not flee. I hid behind my friend—who is taller than I am—and could only barely bring out the words: *He's got a dog!* Some of the other travelers heard me and looked around at me. My face must have been ashen, to judge by the others' faces—but the British are very polite and nobody said a word or asked any question. Before too long, the door to the platform was opened and we were allowed to take our places in the train. I fully expected cattle cars, but, of course, they weren't; they were normal passenger cars. It must have taken me a good half hour to stop trembling and to get my breathing back to normal. What had happened? To this day, I do not know—we never did find out why there was a roped-off area or why the man in uniform had a dog. Westerbork in today's life!

The past intrudes in other ways as well, less frightening, but as clear and as much part of the past. Some years ago I was in a hotel with some friends. In the morning we came down to a lavish breakfast buffet which had everything on it and in it one could possibly desire. Amongst it all were crusty rolls, soft rolls, nut bread, and slices of different breads. One of my friends said, somewhat indignantly: *There is no toast!* My first thought—and I managed to not say it out loud, was: *Be glad you have bread— what more could you want?* Again, Westerbork in today's life! Obviously, my brain tells me that the man with the dog wasn't after *me* personally, but my emotions get in the way. My brain tells me that it is O.K. to want toast—but my ghosts tell me to be content with what I have.

Perhaps because of not having anything, both during the war and for many years after the war, many material things do not matter to me today. Yes, I would be sad and upset if I lost my books—but they are only *things* and can be replaced. I would be sad and upset if I lost my art work; it cannot be replaced but these pieces are only *things*. It doesn't matter to me to which restaurant we go to eat; one is as good as another. If I never went there again, I might be sad, but it is only a *thing*. If I lost my house, I would certainly be sad and upset, but it is also only a *thing* and, with luck, can be replaced. What cannot be replaced, is my life—and I have been lucky enough to have a large number of "bonus years." I was supposed to die as a child; Hitler decided that. But here I am, fifty-seven years after the war and I am still living. My life matters—at least to me. My family photographs matter—at least to me. Neither can be replaced. Somehow and some time—and I do not know just when—I detached from material things and they no longer matter. My friends matter and they cannot be replaced. My cousins, i.e. my family—what is left of it—matters and they cannot be replaced.

There are other things that matter, but they are not material either. What happened, had happened *because* we were Jews. Because we were Jews, we had to wear the yellow star. Because we were Jews we had to be segregated from the rest of the population. Because we were Jews, we were "unworthy of life." Because we were Jews, we were imprisoned in concentration camps. Because we were Jews, we were murdered in gas chambers. Because we were Jews, we were not supposed to survive anywhere. Hitler wanted to make the world "Judenrein," "clean of Jews." He did not succeed. But today, when someone tells me that I am "too sensitive" when I hear an anti-semitic remark or when I am forced to listen to a racist "joke," I get angry. When the 1991 Gulf War started, I said that undoubtedly before long the world would say that it was all the fault of the Jews. I was told that I was "too sensitive." Within three days, the papers said exactly that. So when I am told that, once again, I am "too sensitive," that matters and it makes me angry. It also makes me feel very alone.

Then there is the question of hiding. Many of us survivors survived in hiding, including many of my fellow Child Survivors. When we came out of hiding, the world had changed. Many of us, in some way, are still in hiding. What does that mean? Well, it means that we do not tell our story easily and mostly only if and when we are asked. Many survivors do not want to talk about the past at all; they prefer to "fit in," i.e., to hide. But hiding can be done in other ways, too. At a gathering of friends, someone proposed that we all tell about something that happened to us and that was very frightening and/or life threatening. When my turn came, did I tell anything? No, all I said was: *Nothing life threatening ever happened to me*. Of course, the concentration camp was not at all life threatening! Neither were the soldiers on the street! Or the clandestine foods that we had in the house! Or the transports which took people to "the East" from where they did not come back! Did I say anything about that? Of course not! I hid within myself and not even the friends who have known me for fifty years and know what happened to me reacted to my statement. The only thing someone said was: *How lucky for you*. Most of the time I manage to hide my thoughts, such as: *Be glad you have bread* and manage not to say anything. Others hide other things of the same type. But it is hiding and we cannot seem to get over that. That too, we learn to live with.

Today, in these later years, I am sad for the child I could have been and never was. For the child who was never properly mourned, who "died" but who yet still is but who is not recognized because I am now, after all, an "adult." Neither the child nor the adult know yet how to deal with the "black spot" inside of me, the being a Jew who is not O.K. Neither the child nor the adult know how to deal with the memory blanks which are still there and can't be filled in. Neither the child nor the adult know how to deal with the old pain which never goes away and is yet so new. Neither the child nor the adult know how to deal with the questions people ask sometimes: *What was it like in the concentration camps? Were you ever afraid? Did you see people shot? Did you see people die?* How does one answer these questions? How many years have you got to listen to the answer? How many years have I got to tell the answer?

Residuals—The Present

In a number of chapters I have told about feeling different. In 2001, I wrote a poem about this; here it is.

DIFFERENT

So often, when I am with others
I feel myself different from them.
I ask myself:
"Why am I different?"
"How am I different?"

I am European,
but live in the USA.
Am I a hyphenated person
rather than a whole one?
English is not my first language,
yet I speak it day by day
albeit with an accent.
I will always be a foreigner.

I am a Jew
in a mostly Christian country,
and am told
that I am "too sensitive"
on subjects concerning Jews.

I am a Holocaust survivor
living in a country
whose population
has not known war intimately
since the War Between the States
and when it did experience war,
after 1865,
that war was far away—
too far to really know it.

I don't laugh
at the same jokes
as others do
because I do not deem them funny.
People say that
my sense of humor is "strange."
I don't consider it strange,
I think it may be European.
Europe is, after all,
my origin.

People ask me questions:
"Where are you from?"
"What accent do you have?"
"Why did you come here?"
I rarely, if ever,
ask such personal questions
and people judge that strange.
I do not think it strange,
I believe it's not my business.

I do not smile or laugh
as easily as others do;
I find it difficult
to be boisterous.
When I was a teenager
my classmates called me "sloom"*
"dull" they said, "slow" and "boring."
They said I was too serious.
I think that maybe
this has not changed.

In all these ways,
am I different:
different for all these reasons.
Over the years
I've learned to live with it.
Only on some days
I feel it more
than on others.

* *sloom*—Dutch word, meaning slow, boring, dull

What that all really means is that I think I can never really fit in. I had, at one time, a cousin who lived in England. She and her husband had fled there, from Germany. They had a good life, a productive life, a life they liked. They had been helped to come by the Quakers and after long thought, both she and her husband became Quakers. She never regretted it. But one day, some forty years after my cousin had come to England, she told me:

You know, I never will fit in here. I no longer feel German, but I do not feel English. I speak both German and English fluently, but I have an accent. I do not feel Jewish, but I also do not feel Christian. I am neither fish nor fowl.

That explains it as clearly as anything does. It has nothing, actually, to do with being Jewish. It has more to do, I think, with being an immigrant. You can learn customs, songs, games, how to celebrate holidays, you can learn the language of the country. But nobody will ever let you forget that you are an immigrant, that you are different. Often this comes out by way of compliments: *You speak English so well. You don't have an accent.* Still it emphasizes the difference. It has taken me most of my life to find out that you can never fit in. That too, one learns to live with. Those of us who, like me, survived the Holocaust, have often lived or temporarily resided in many different countries. I was born in Germany, lived there my first five years. Then we moved to Amsterdam, Holland, which meant learning a new language and new customs. While we were living there, we were declared stateless, because Hitler said that every Jew who had left Germany could not retain the German nationality. Then came the war and the Holocaust and we were deported to first one and then another concentration camp. After the war, we returned to Holland, a Holland which was very different from what it had been. Then came my time in Denmark—yet another language I didn't understand and customs I knew nothing about. Back to Holland after three months. In about 1953 or '54 my parents moved (temporarily!) to London, England where they stayed for ten years, after which they moved (again temporarily!) to Zurich, Switzerland, where, after about sixteen years, they eventually died. Meanwhile I had moved to the USA. Is it any wonder I sometimes feel dislocated? Of course, I am not the only one—this happened to many survivor families. But I can only speak truly about myself.

During my teen years and early twenties, everything I did well or had a talent for, or any good physical quality, always came from someone else. My parents used to tell me that I had my good teeth from my father, my face from my mother since I resembled her so much. I was good at languages because my mother and grandmother were good at them. My intelligence came from my father. Somehow nothing was ever originally *mine*. I found it very hurtful at the time, though it was not meant that way. But it made me feel that in and of myself I was nothing. And if I am nothing, do I then really exist? Yet, in these, my later years, I have found out that my history is mine, my story is mine, my feelings are mine, my intelligence is mine, my memory is mine. It was one of the many revelations that came through both therapy and the contact with the Child Survivors. That contact continues, naturally. We have been together now, as a group of Child Survivors, since 1983. As of 1988, we have had get-togethers, called conferences, every year in different locations, so that everyone, in any state or country, has a chance to attend. As a result, we now have a family of sisters and brothers that we never had before. Many of us have been orphans since childhood. Many of us have no blood sisters or brothers. But we now have siblings—whom one of us called "phantom siblings"—and we enjoy each other as much as we help each other. We gather in hotels, usually, but the places in which we gather become different from other places. Here is a poem I wrote in 1999, after one of our conferences.

A DIFFERENT PLACE

Once again we welcome each other,
we, Jewish children of the Holocaust,
at a Child Survivors' Conference,
for the ninth time in nine years.
When we arrive,
wherever we come from,
we come to be with family,
our family of choice.
This place, wherever it is,
becomes a different place,
a magical place,
a sacred place—
for here we all belong.

We all understand
that we are children,
children who lost our childhood,
children now grown up,
with the memories of adults,
adults with no memories of being children.
Here, now, this is a different world:
a world of childhood and play,
now, when we are growing older.
A world of middle or old age,
now, when we are learning how to play.

We are closer to each other
than to our other family:
spouses, daughters, sons.
We know each other less
but we understand each other more.
The same shadows lurk in our eyes,
the same sun shines from our smiles,
even while tears course down our cheeks.
We are a living miracle
because we are still here,
because we are able to live
today as well as yesterday and tomorrow
though we were not supposed to live at all.
We look backward to the past,
we look forward to the future
in one and the same glance.
We are perhaps not whole,
but we are wholly human.
The miracle is that we *are*.

We carry the same heavy burden
but we dance joyfully;
when we are all together,
we unshroud the child within.
As we slowly grow older,
our burden grows no lighter
but it is shared among many of us.
We are blessed by each other,
and by each other's presence.
We not only feel *for* each other,
but also *with* each other.
The feelings of one of us
are those of all of us
though we may only just have met.

Here we are not outsiders,
we are not strangers,
are not "eccentric,"
not "peculiar," not "odd."
Here we are not told to forget
because it's all so long ago;
not told we were "only" children
and therefore did not suffer,
cannot remember and do not know.
Here we are with kinfolk,
long lost or never had,
here we are siblings
though we have not the same parents,
here, at last, we belong.

Between us, between Child Survivors, communication is often unspoken. The Second Generation (i.e the children of Survivors, born after the war) has that same bond amongst themselves. All our parents spoke about the past either far too much or not at all. Most of us, whose parents did not speak about the past, were left to find things out on our own. It took many years to do that. It took many years to find possible birth brothers or sisters who might have survived. It took many years to re-establish contact with hiding families who had hidden children whose birth parents later forbade any contact. It took many years to find out that we did understand, did know, did suffer and do remember. It took many years to find our Child Survivor siblings, but now the bond is strong. Yes, we quarrel occasionally—what siblings don't? No, we don't always agree on everything—what siblings do? And as we continue to get together and to remain in contact, our bond will grow even stronger because now we have a family to whom we truly belong.

☞ *Important Things Today*

There are a number of things which are important to me today. Some are material (in spite of the detachment!), some are not. It is really important to me that I have enough food in the house; not just enough for today or for the whole week, but a certain supply for an indetermined time, just in case.... It is equally important that I have enough toilet paper and soap in the house, again: a supply. The former was nonexistent in the camp and the latter was very, very scarce. Cleaning products, equally nonexistent in the camp, are also of inportance. If I don't have these things or see that I am about to run out of them, I get very nervous and the need to go to the store over-whelms me.

The unlimited possibility of warm water, a warm bath or a hot shower are also important. None of those existed in the camps and it is still a miracle that I now have them. The possibility of going where I want and when I want is also important. In the concentration camps I was behind barbed wire, imprisoned, I could not go anywhere. Now it is just the opposite and it makes me feel really free.

Another important thing is the freedom of fear of death. I am not afraid to die. Perhaps in the camps I was so close to death that Death became a sort of person, someone not to fear, but someone always present. Should something happen to me, as it can anytime and anywhere, well, then so be it. I do not go around looking for death, I do not invite Death into my house or into my presence, but neither am I afraid of Death.

So that brings me to the non-material things. One of those things is bearing witness. I do this by going to schools and also other groups to speak of my experiences. I lecture—speak, whatever you want to call it, for whomever wants me to come. For any school in my area, for any class whose teacher calls me and asks me, I will go there to tell my story. Often people ask me to talk about "The Holocaust." That is impossible; it would take years to discuss everything and I am not an expert on everything that happened in every country. I *am*, however, an expert on my own story. Usually, the teacher has already presented a long program of lectures, readings, films, research and the like. When I come to speak, I am a witness. I was there, I saw it, I know it happened. Nobody can tell me that there was no Holocaust, that Jews were not murdered. I was there. So I tell the students that I was a child, how old I was, what happened and when. They usually have a lot of questions and I leave time for those. Interestingly, the lower the grade level, the more questions the students ask. Sometimes, if I have enough time, I will read some of my poetry. That also depends on the level of the class. Obviously, I cannot speak the same way in a fifth-grade class and a twelfth-grade class. Some classes make drawings. Some students want their picture taken with me. Some want to shake my hand. Some are just amazed that someone from that faraway time is still actually alive and can visit. These visits and lectures are extremely important to me. Why? Well, once my generation of Child Survivors is gone, there will be no witnesses left. There will be video and audio tapes, yes, but no living witnesses. So while I can, I want to bear witness that the Holocaust happened, that it was a real thing and that it can happen again wherever the time and the climate are ripe. I speak out against prejudice in my talks, as well, because that belongs with it. In my time, it was prejudice against

Gabriele in class, 1999.

Gabriele with students after a lecture on her experiences, 2000.

180   IS THE WAR OVER?

Jews—and that hasn't changed; it still exists—but there are other prejudices: by whites against people with another skin color, people with perhaps another eye shape. Prejudices by healthy people against those who are handicapped: have you never seen a person in a wheelchair, maybe in a restaurant? The server often asks the person pushing the wheelchair: "What does he (or she) want?" My answer to that is: "Why don't you ask him (or her)?" Just because a person cannot walk, does not mean that that person cannot hear or answer a question! There are all kinds of prejudices and they must all be rooted out, if that is possible. The memories we (i.e. we Holocaust survivors) have cannot be let be; they won't stay away in any event as you have seen in this book. I feel a need to pass on these memories. History comes alive if someone was there and can say: "I was there." I feel it as an obligation to speak out, though in actual fact, it is not an obligation for me but a need. The need becomes greater as I get older. Our time is finite; if I don't speak out now, then who will do it? In a way, it is also a proof to myself that I do not live *in* the past, though, of course, I do live *with* it. That means that I can take it out and look at it, when it suits *me*, not just when it comes out all by itself. I believe that we cannot afford indifference. If we, who lived it, do not speak out, then who will?

I also feel a strong need to stand up for those children who did not survive, the one and a half million children who were murdered. They cannot speak for themselves; one of us has to do it. So I do it. I am not taking on their lives, but they did live at one time. They were individuals, not an amorphous mass of children. That needs to be shown. I wrote a poem about these children in 1992, choosing as the title the name my fellow Child Survivor invented, though I use it in a different meaning:

PHANTOM SIBLINGS

Wherever my life's path leads me,
I am never alone,
a throng of phantom children stays close by me.
They precede me, faces turned rearward,
follow me, hands stretched towards me,
float all around me
like a cloud of tears.
They wait, ever hopeful for remembrance;
their patience knows no end.

Their bodies were murdered long ago
during the Holocaust years:
now their shades accompany me—
ghostly images of their living selves.
Some are naked,
small ribs edging through their grimy skin,
faces evincing fear.
Others are dressed in tatters,
barely veiling hunger-swollen bellies,
pale faces pleading for compassion.
Others yet are clad in colorful clothes,
school satchels still on their backs,
a laugh still on their lips.
I know none of them by name,
I know all of them by sufferings.
Each Friday night I recite Kaddish *
for all these tiny phantoms.
I would need a million million years
to say Kaddish for every single soul,
so they must share their Kaddish.

Kaddish—Hebrew. Literally: sanctification. It is a prayer
customarily recited by mourners.

They know this, they accept it
by their journeying with me
who so almost was one of them.

They depend on me,
they depend on us all
who were children then,
children just like them.
They count on us, on me
for we are all they have.

I am accustomed to their company,
have grown to love them,
would be lonely without them.
I am responsible for them,
they are my sisters, brothers, family.
Did they die in my stead?
They are part of me
as I am part of them;
they live with me
as I died with them.
Reciting Kaddish for my phantom siblings
is one way of giving thanks
that I am still alive.

Lecturing, then, is part of the legacy I wish to leave. Another part of that legacy consists of video tapes and audio tapes telling my story, which I have made for various museums and organizations. After I die, at least there will still be those tapes to tell the story. It isn't as good as a live witness, but it is a whole lot better than no witness at all.

⌒ *Is the War Over?*

So, is the war over? Really, truly over? Obviously, the fighting of World War II is over and has been for a long time. But what about for those who lived through it? Again: I can only speak for myself, perhaps a little for my parents, but certainly not for anyone else.

The numbness which had begun with the persecution of us Jews lasted a long time, in fact, many years. For a very long time, I could not "open the door to myself." I was afraid to even try it, because experience had shown me that nobody wanted to hear. It was also far too painful for me to talk or write about. I thought that if I tried to open that door, I would start to cry and I would never stop again; I would drown in my own tears. There were so many losses: my grandparents, all of their siblings and all the descendants of those siblings, all the friends I had made in my German childhood and all those whom I had made a little later in my Dutch childhood. There were other losses as well: the environment to which I was used as a small child; the contacts with family, e.g. the cousins of my father and mother. I lost my first language, German, in the sense that it was not spoken—as a national language—in Holland, that it became a language of which to be frightened because it was the "official" Nazi language and concentration camp language.

I lost my toys which, to a child, are very important. I lost my privacy. My mother and father lost all of their family and friends, their possessions, as well as their language and their privacy. Just as I felt, after the war, that I had lost myself, my parents may well have felt the same. If I opened the above-mentioned door, all of this would come falling out, all of it would have to be mourned and I knew then that I was not capable of that. Not yet. So it was better, safer, not to try. Eventually, thanks to a very good therapist, I was able to open that door to myself and look inside and deal with what I found there. I was able with her help to mourn my losses. I was able to look at what had happened and think about it and get rid of the ideas which had been put into my head that we "really hadn't had it so bad." After all, Theresienstadt was touted (by the Nazis) as a "ghetto," not a concentration camp. A ghetto for those Jews who were privileged. This, of course, is not the truth at all, Theresienstadt was a concentration camp and the "privilege" needs to be taken with many a grain of salt. Is it a privilege to be starved? Is it a privilege to be beaten? Is it a privilege to be worked to death? Is it a privilege to be always cold? Is it a privilege to have no soap and no toilet paper? Those privileges, I can do without!

It is still very difficult to talk about those years and those experiences. But nowadays I can open the door at will and close it at will. That means that when I speak to a class of students or another group, I can distance myself from what I tell. Usually it—the subject—catches up with me when I return home and manifests itself as enormous fatigue.

What hasn't gone away, is the feeling of being different, of never fitting in completely. What has also not gone away, is the striving to do the best I can in anything I do. That feeling was present even in Elementary School, after the war, and it has never left me. I had to do my absolute best, I thought. For whom? I don't know. My parents did not require it. I think it has to do with the feeling of having a "flaw" that I had as a child and a young girl. If I just did my absolute best, it would make up for the flaw. The habit of doing the best I can do has never left me.

Mostly, today, the war isn't over because there are too many "outside stimuli" (my word for these things) which set off memories. There are sounds: police sirens, firefighters' sirens, even the booming of fireworks. There are smells and visions: in an earlier chapter I gave the example of the umbrella which I took to be a gun. There was also the time when, from a motel window, I saw two very tall chimneys with flames on top. That time also I must have turned ashen, because some people who were with me, gave me some very strange looks. Naturally I did not explain anything—after all, I'm still in hiding, and besides, in order to tell what had scared me, I would have to go back deep into the past. I cannot do that from my hiding place. There are touches: either the touch of a material I don't like (usually because it reminds me of something I may have worn in the camp) or someone's touching me when I haven't seen that person coming. A sudden ringing of the bell makes me shiver. Sometimes these things are my interpretation, sometimes they are not. One evening, a long time ago, I smelled gas in the house. I checked everywhere, but could not find any leak. I called the Gas Company; someone came. There was nothing to find. I had lit a Yahrzeit light (a candle which is lit on the anniversary of someone's death) for a friend who had been murdered in the gas chambers. The gas smell wasn't there; it was simply my perception.

Although I can read memoirs and other books about the Holocaust, I can never bring myself to go to see a movie or a play about it, or even a war movie which has nothing to do with the Holocaust. Movies make situations very much alive; I get too involved in them. It then seems to me that I am *in* the situation and that frightens me; the past has come back. So I avoid that type of movie. I can't afford to see them: the consequence is either a week's worth of nightmares or a migraine which lasts for days. To give an example: there was a movie a few years ago about a young boy in the Blitz of London. (I have, not unexpectedly, forgotten the name of the movie.) In it was a scene during which the mother of the boy put tape, packaging tape, on the windows of their house, so that falling bombs would not shatter the windows. I remember that very well from when my mother and grandmother did it. In that darkened theater, I whispered to the mother: *No, no, that's the wrong kind of tape. It has to be wider, or else it won't help!*

That's what I mean when I say that I get too involved in the situation.

Sometimes people ask me what life would have been like if there had been no Holocaust. I can't answer that, of course, because, after all, there *was* the Holocaust. But there are some things I know: my parents would have had more children. Both my parents had a sibling and they wanted more than one child. But I was born in the year in which Hitler came to power. By the time my parents had regained their health and we might have been able to afford another baby, it was too late. Just as there are residuals for me, there were residuals for my parents. My father could never stand the ringing of the bell or a sudden telephone call. After the war, he never slept well again: there was no single night in which he slept the whole night through. He also wanted to control whatever he could control. Therefore his desk was always perfectly clean or else he had the papers lined up just so; the postage stamps in one particular drawer and everything in its place. Whatever could be planned ahead was planned in detail. Nothing was left to chance. My mother was not like that but, after the war, she never laughed aloud again, at most she smiled. Both of them had the same habit I have: a goodly supply of food had to be in the house. The three of us were a very close-knit family: we could talk about anything and everything, except, as mentioned, the war and the Holocaust. I found it totally natural to go to my mother or my father with whatever problem I might have. However, just as they never wanted to worry me, so I never wanted to worry them. As a result, there were things which perhaps should have been talked about but weren't.

So, is the war over? No, it isn't, not for me and not for those other Child Survivors whom I know. It will never be over. Our ghosts will always be with us; our memories will always be there, our idiosyncrasies will always come out and, even though we are now growing old, we will always be children—the children we were never allowed to be in reality.

Let me end with yet another poem which describes the difference between the years after the war and now.

THEN AND NOW

It was in June
nineteen fory-five
that we returned
to Amsterdam
from the concentration camps
where we had been imprisoned
for two years.

On our arrival
our pre-war neighbors
embraced us welcomingly
and we lived with them
for at least a year,
before we could move back
into our pre-war apartment.

Those first years
after the war,
there was not much
of anything:
clothing, coal, food, housing,
to be had in Holland.

Though food was very scarce,
yet they shared all they had,
and it stretched for all of us.
It was simple food
but given generously
and eaten in freedom.

We took no baths
and no showers
unless we wanted them cold.
We washed in the washbasin
in ice cold water
that was only sometimes
halfway lukewarm
if we had heated a kettle.

Eventually,
when times got better,
there was hot water
once a week
and we took our baths
in six inches of water.

When winter came,
there was no heat
because there was no coal
to heat the furnace.
We wore more clothes,
if we had them,
to try and keep warm.
Eventually,
when times got better,
we had some heat
some of the time.

In my room
with its North-East exposure,
there was a tiny
metal radiator.
It was called central heating
but it warmed only
the corner where it stood.
I put a pillow on it
and sat on that
to keep warm
while doing my homework.

Several years later
we had hot water
every day.
A warm bath a day,
in a full tub,
what luxury!

Then also our radiators
produced more heat
because there was more coal.
The house was warm
except my room
with its North-East exposure.
To keep warm,
I did my homework in bed.

Today
I have a warm house,
with hot water
all the time.
I can have
all the heat I want
all the time,
and all the showers
or baths I want,
any time.

I have warm clothes
any time I need them,
and enough food to eat
every day.
What more could I
possibly want?

⌇ *Epilogue*

So, is the war over? Really over? The fighting stopped when I was twelve, but the war was not over. I could tell, even at that age, that the adults in my life were anxious, nervous perhaps. They would stop talking when I came into the room. I could tell, even at that age that they were often afraid, but were trying not to show it. I didn't know what they were afraid of, but I knew that it had to be the same sort of afraid as I felt. I didn't know what I was afraid of, either.

The first years after the war were difficult for everyone. Nobody had anything much, the country needed rebuilding, the cities needed rebuilding, there was not enough housing; everybody was deprived of most things. But those years were perhaps doubly or triply difficult for Jewish survivors. In addition to what the everyday citizens did not have, the survivors had also lost all their family and all their possessions. They—we— couldn't talk about what they—we—had endured. That, perhaps, was the principal difference between us survivors and the rest of the population.

Since I felt that I was different, my parents probably felt the same. They never talked about it. But that feeling meant that the war was not over. Not only did I not fit in, my parents and other adults didn't either. To top it all off, they—we—were immigrants; my parents spoke with an accent. I did not hear it anymore, but others did.

All of us had and have memories. Since mine haven't "gone away," I feel sure that my parents' memories didn't disappear either. These memories will never go away. They are pictures in my mind, as clear today as when the actual events happened. The pictures will never dim. As I have mentioned before, the ghosts will never disappear. They will always want to "come out," to be with me. They would like to possess me, but I will not let them. Memories do strange things; they make you see things which aren't visible, make you hear sounds which aren't audible, make you taste things which aren't on your plate, make you smell odors which cannot be scented.

And what do we do with our memories? Or rather, what do I do, since I cannot speak for anyone else. I write them down, as I have in my previous books and in this book. I try to be as precise as possible, I try to explain what cannot truly be explained. I also speak about them, to school groups and others. Some people think that this is all "therapeutic." It is not. It is as difficult now as it was the first time. It will be as difficult the next time as it is now. It will always be like the first time.

The war is *not* over and it will never be—not for me and not for those other Child Survivors whom I know. It has wounded us with wounds which did not heal well if at all. We have ugly scars which cannot be seen, but which are nevertheless there. We can feel them. We are growing older, yet still feel like children. We have children of our own, yet feel as though we never grew up. Just as we were 150 years old when we were twelve, we are now, in our older or old age, children still. No, the war is *not* over and it never will be.

What Happened to Whom?

My Immediate Family

Gertrud Teppich (née Herz), my maternal grandmother, committed suicide in November 1942, when she was on the point of being deported to Auschwitz.

Ernst Silten, my paternal grandfather, committed suicide in March 1943, when the Nazis were knocking on his door to deport him to Auschwitz.

Marta Silten (née Friedberg), my paternal grandmother, committed suicide in July 1943 in the concentration camp Westerbork (Holland) when her name appeared on a list of people to be deported to Auschwitz.

Fritz Silten, my father, survived Westerbork (Holland) and Theresienstadt (Czechoslovakia). He died in November 1980.

Ilse Silten (née Teppich), my mother, survived Westerbork (Holland) and Theresienstadt (Czechoslovakia). She died in February 1977.

Ursula (Ulle) Teppich, my aunt, my mother's sister, went to Switzerland in 1938 and lived there for the rest of her life. She died in May 1990.

Heinz (Henry) Silten, my uncle, my father's brother, went to England in the mid-thirties and lived there for the rest of his life. He died in March 1953.

R. Gabriele S. Silten, I, the author of this book, survived Westerbork (Holland) and Theresienstadt (Czechoslovakia). I finished Elementary School after the war, in Amsterdam (Holland) and went to High School there. I came to the USA in February 1959 and have lived here since then.

Other Family, Friends and Acquaintances

Carla, my upstairs neighbor and friend, as well as her sister **Willy** and their parents **Tante Trien** and **Oom Wim** survived the war in Amsterdam (Holland). Tante Trien and Oom Wim have died, but Carla and Willy live in Holland today.

Uncle Hans and his son **Erik. Uncle Hans** was my father's first cousin, though I called him "uncle." He lived in Denmark, was taken over to Sweden during the war and survived there. He returned to Denmark and died there in 1970. His son Erik is still alive at this writing and lives in Denmark. Uncle Hans also had a daughter, Anethe, well after the war; she lives in Denmark with her son.

Edith, my friend and study mate survived the war in hiding. She still lives in Holland.

Mr. and Mrs. Katz, my parents' friends, lived in Amsterdam, Holland after the war and died there.

Elisa, my friend since Geneva, finished her studies there and returned to Portugal. She still lives in Portugal.

Mr. and Mrs. Van der Guus, my parents' friends, survived the war in Holland. We became friends after the war; they were my "landlords" for a while. They lived in Holland and eventually died there.

Fred and Jetty Benjamin, my parents' friends, survived the war in various concentration camps. They emigrated to the

USA after the war, lived on the East coast to begin with and later, after their retirement, on the West coast. Fred died in 1959; Jetty died in 1986.

Hans, my one and only friend in Theresienstadt. He was a couple of years younger than I; we were inseparable. In November of 1944, **Hans,** his brother **Werner** and their parents, **Eduard** and **Suzanne,** were deported from Theresienstadt to Auschwitz and gassed there on arrival.

Max, my childhood friend from first and second grade, survived the war with his parents, in hiding. His father died shortly after the war. **Max** and his mother emigrated to the USA, where **Max** still lives today.

Glossary

buiten (Dutch): outside

ça, s'il vous plaît (French): that, please

Dag Mevrouw (Dutch): good evening/morning, Ma'am

Dank U wel Mevrouw (Dutch): thank you, Ma'am

Eindhoven (Dutch): a city in Holland

fout (Dutch): wrong, incorrect

foute ouders (Dutch): "wrong" parents, i.e. parents who collaborated with the Nazis

griffel (Dutch): slate pencil

griffeldoos (Dutch): box to keep slate pencils in

Hongerwinter (Dutch): Hungerwinter, i.e. the winter of 1944–1945

Judenfrei (German): free of Jews

Judenrein (German): cleansed of Jews

Kaddish (Hebrew): literally, sanctification. It is a prayer customarily recited by mourners

Kleiderkammer (German): clothing warehouse

La vieille ville (French): the old city, old town

lei (Dutch): slate

lyceum (Dutch): a type of Dutch school

Madame (French): Mrs., Ma'am

mag (Dutch): may

Mag Gaby buiten spelen? (Dutch): May Gaby come outside and play?

Maison des Etudiants (French): Students' House

Mevrouw (Dutch): Mrs., Ma'am

Mijnheer (Dutch): Mr., Sir

Nationaal Socialistische Bond (NSB) The name of the Dutch Nazi party

Oom (Dutch): Uncle

ouders (Dutch): parents

sloom (Dutch): slow, dull, boring

spelen (Dutch): play (verb)

Tante (Dutch): Aunt

Theresienstadt (German): a concentration camp in Czechoslovakia

Terezín (Czech): same camp as above

Westerbork (Dutch): a concentration camp in Holland

Zauberberg (German): *The Magic Mountain*, title of a novel by Thomas Mann